The Moscow Lectures on Psychoanalysis

The Moscow Lectures on Psychoanalysis

Edited by
Arnold Rothstein, M.D.

International Universities Press, Inc.
Madison Connecticut

Library of Congress Cataloging-in-Publication Data

The Moscow lectures and psychoanalysis / edited by Arnold Rothstein.
p. cm.
Consists of papers presented at seminars in Moscow in Apr. 1990.
Includes bibliographical references and index.
ISBN 0-8236-3435-3
1. Psychoanalysis—Congresses. 2. Freud, Sigmund, 1856-1939—-Congresses. I. Rothstein, Arnold, 1936-
[DNLM: 1. Freudian Theory—congresses. 2. Psychoanalysis—-congresses. 3. Psychotherapy—congresses. WM 460 M8965 1990]
RC500.5.M67 1991
616.89'17—dc20
DNLM/DLC
for Library of Congress 91-30974
CIP

Manufactured in the United States of America

Contents

Contributors

Sander M. Abend, M.D., Training and Supervising Analyst, New York Psychoanalytic Institute; Editor-in-Chief, *Psychoanalytic Quarterly*.

Dale Boesky, M.D., Training and Supervising Analyst, Michigan Psychoanalytic Institute; past Editor-in-Chief, *The Psychoanalytic Quarterly*.

Charles Brenner, M.D., Training and Supervising Analyst, New York Psychoanalytic Institute; Past President, American Psychoanalytic Association; author, *An Elementary Textbook of Psychoanalysis, Psychoanalytic Technique and Psychic Conflict*, and *The Mind in Conflict*.

Homer C. Curtis, M.D., Training and Supervising Analyst, Institute of the Philadelphia Association for Psychoanalysis; Past President, American Psychoanalytic Association.

Scott Dowling, M.D., Faculty, Cleveland Psychoanalytic Institute; Editor, *The Psychoanalytic Study of the Child* and *The Workshop Series of the American Psychoanalytic Association*.

Arnold Rothstein, M.D., Clinical Professor of Psychiatry, Mt. Sinai School of Medicine; Member, New York Psychoanalytic Society; Founding Editor, *Workshop Series of the American Psychoanalytic Association*; Co-editor, *On Beginning An Analysis*; author, *The Narcissistic Pursuit of Perfection* and *The Structural Hypothesis: An Evolutionary Perspective*.

Preface

In 1987, in response to *glasnost*, I mentioned to Martin Azarian that it seemed timely to organize a group of colleagues to conduct seminars in the Soviet Union on the fundamentals of psychoanalysis. In June 1989, Mr. Azarian told me that Dr. Marat Vartanian, the Director of the National Mental Health Research Center of the Soviet Union, the Russian equivalent of the U.S. National Institute of Mental Health, was coming to the United States and would enjoy discussing possible scientific exchanges.

On June 21st, 1989, Sander Abend and I met with Dr. Vartanian. (Dr. Abend was acting in his capacity as Secretary of the American Psychoanalytic Association, and as the representative of its President, Homer Curtis.) In response to an outline of my ideas, Dr. Vartanian remarked that Soviet mental health workers knew very little about psychoanalysis because prior to *glasnost* and *perestroika* the idea of the unconscious had been "outlawed." Dr. Vartanian invited me to develop a proposed curriculum to be taught by a group of American psychoanalysts at the National Mental Health Research Center in Moscow in 1990. The invitation was historic in that it represented the first formal invitation in sixty years to western psychoanalysts to teach psychoanalysis within the institution of Soviet psychiatry.

On October 14th, 1989, the Executive Committee of the American Psychoanalytic Association enthusiastically agreed to accept the invitation. In April 1990, Drs. Sander Abend, Homer Curtis, Scott Dowling, and myself went to the Soviet Union to conduct seminars in psychoanalysis and to meet with Soviet colleagues in the mental health field, some of whom were themselves interested in using psychoanalytic concepts with their patients.

Before proceeding it is worth noting that from the inception of this project, in the summer of 1989, we were concerned with the question of the correctness of collaborating with leading representatives of Soviet psychiatry, in view of the significant human rights abuses of which Soviet psychiatry has been accused. Ultimately we decided to follow the lead of other western scientists and professionals: We decided to look to the future instead of the past. We judged that our visit would represent a contribution to the development of psychoanalysis in the Soviet Union, and our experience confirmed these hopeful expectations.

In addition to the formal lectures, significant and satisfying contacts were made with Soviet psychiatrists, psychologists, and academics interested in psychoanalysis.

Three exchanges were particularly noteworthy. On April 24th, 1990, we had a formal debate with three leading Soviet neuropsychologists working in the tradition of Pavlov: Professors N. Bekhtereva, P. Semonov, and M. Yaroshevsky. In our exchange it became clear that both groups were asking similar questions. Academician Seminov (1986), in his book *The Emotional Brain,* asks, "What is 'personality' " (p. 4). In addition he states, "we are concerned with . . . something else hidden behind the facade of emotional feelings" (p. 7). In our exchanges Dr. Curtis emphasized that the psychoanalytic method was uniquely suited to contribute to an understanding of these questions.

A second important exchange centered around the visit of Drs. Curtis and Dowling, on April 25th, 1990, to the National Center of Psychoneuroendocrinology. This is a clinic under the direction of Professor Aron J. Belkin.

Drs. Curtis and Dowling met with Dr. Belkin, Dr. Lev Gertsik, and seventeen other interested colleagues. They discussed clinical material late into the evening. It is noteworthy that Dr. Belkin is the President of the newly organized Soviet Psychoanalytic Society and the editor of a recently published Russian translation of *Selected Writings of Sigmund Freud*, the entire first printing of which (130,000 copies) was sold in four days.

Finally, in Leningrad, we met Dr. Modest M. Kabanov and Dr. Yuri Popov, the Director and Associate Director respectively of the Bekhterev Institute. We had a very satisfying exchange with them and with twenty members of the staff of the Institute's outpatient psychotherapy clinic. All of these exchanges impressed us with our Soviet colleagues' enormous interest in psychoanalysis.

Arnold Rothstein
August 1990

Introduction

Arnold Rothstein, M.D.

These lectures on psychoanalysis are intended to provide an introduction to the subject. They describe both the development and contemporary status of Freudian psychoanalysis.

In Chapter 1, Abend chronicles Freud's early discoveries in terms of the psychoanalytic method, the unconscious, and of the importance of the fantasies and conflicts associated with infantile sexual development, all of which provided a revolutionary new perspective on human motivation. Freud's investigations proposed new understandings of symptoms, dreams, and the therapeutic relationship.

In Chapter 2, Abend describes Freud's major theoretical reformulations at the age of seventy. After describing Freud's topographic model, Abend delineates his reformulations as responses to the lessons of clinical experience. That experience, particularly with depressed, self-destructive, and self-defeating patients, complemented Freud's increasing appreciation of unconscious aspects of defensive functioning and of conflicts related to hostile drive derivatives and unconscious wishes for punishment. The result of this experience was Freud's proposal of the structural theory and the related signal theory of anxiety.

I conceived of the third lecture as an outline summary of Brenner's (1982) *The Mind in Conflict*. Because Dr. Brenner had presented just such a lecture, we decided to use it as the third chapter of this book. The emphasis of this chapter is on the ubiquity of conflict concerning infantile sexual wishes in mental life. Brenner states, "The conflicts of childhood determine those of all adult life. The anxieties of adult life . . . and its depressive moods and affects are the consequences, *the echoes*, of those in early childhood" (p. 46; emphasis added).

The fourth and fifth chapters, by myself and Dr. Boesky respectively, present applications of the theory presented in Chapter 3 to varieties of clinical phenomena.

In Chapter 6, Dr. Curtis delineates the distinction between psychoanalysis and varieties of psychotherapy. Curtis suggests that psychotherapy emphasizes "alleviation, relief, adjustment and return to function" (p. 86), while psychoanalysis emphasizes "increased self-knowledge and capacity to continuously expand the awareness of the inner psychic life" (p. 86). This author's emphasis is on the attainment and future employment of the analysand's capacity for self-analysis.

Curtis stresses that "A major contribution of psychoanalysis not only to psychotherapy but also to the field of psychiatry, indeed the whole field of medicine, is the psychodynamic way of thinking" (p. 87).

The study of suffering adults, employing the analytic method, was and remains the fundamental data base of psychoanalysis. However, the central emphasis of a psychoanalytic understanding of normal development and pathogenesis is on conflicts concerning early childhood sexuality.

The study of suffering as well as normal children by a variety of techniques has been an important and expanding analytic concern. In Chapters 7 and 8 Dowling describes the development of child psychoanalysis from the pioneering contributions of Anna Freud, Melanie Klein, and Berta Bornstein to its current status. Dowling emphasizes the profoundly humanistic foundations of the work and its applications. In regard to the child analyst's attitude toward the child, Dowling states: "The child and his utterances are treated with seriousness and respect, often for the first time in his life" (p. 114).

Finally Dowling stresses the importance of the applications of a child analytic perspective to the observational studies of child development. These studies have contributed to a better understanding of normal and pathological development and to the development of more sensitive and sophisticated services for infants and for sick and handicapped children.

The final chapter of this book is dedicated to a further application of the theory of conflict and compromise formation: its application to the treatment of "sicker" patients. This chapter provides the reader with a contemporary Freudian perspective on these patients. The view presented in this chapter is in contrast to the psychiatric perspective, typified by *The Diagnostic and Statistical Manual of Mental Disorders* (DSM-III), that stresses precise descriptive criteria for diagnosis. As Abend notes, "psychoanalytic diagnosis is less precise" (p. 137). This is, in part, because analysts are interested in understanding and interpreting the meanings of behavior rather than in describing its manifest appearance. Such an analytic perspective results in analysts experiencing patients as more similar than different.

The view presented in this chapter is also in significant contrast with other popular psychoanalytic perspectives. A number of important psychoanalytic contributors such as Kohut (1977), Kernberg (1975), Adler (1985), Robbins (1983), and others conceive of sicker patients as suffering the results of trauma that occurred in the first year or two of life. These sicker and more disturbed patients are often discussed from the perspective of a number of diagnostic labels such as *primitive, narcissistic,* and *borderline.* The latter term, popularized by Kernberg, is perhaps the most common designation associated with these patients.

The application of the theory of conflict and compromise formation presented in this final chapter is, in a sense, beyond the usual "borderline" concept. It conceives of these patients as a heterogeneous group. In regard to psychological factors that contribute to severe pathology, a view is presented that counters the emphasis on very early trauma and instead stresses the role of continuing trauma and conflict throughout the developmental phases.

Chapter 1

Freud: The Early Discoveries and the Beginning of the Psychoanalytic Movement

Sander M. Abend, M.D.

In one of several autobiographical summaries of his life work Freud, borrowing a phrase from Hebbel's play *Gyges und sein Ring*, called himself "one of those who have disturbed the sleep of the world."* He went on to predict that he could not count on objectivity and tolerance for his ideas, a prediction that history has since proven to be correct. When a scientist's work arouses continuing, widespread controversy within the broad intellectual community beyond the boundaries of his own particular specialty, it is reasonable to assume that it has somehow, albeit unintentionally, disrupted an important aspect of the human race's usual way of thinking about itself. Other examples that come to mind are Galileo's clear proofs of the

*See Freud, 1914, *Standard Edition, Volume 14*, p. 21.

Copernican revision of cosmography, and Darwin's demonstration that humans are descended by evolution from the lower species, and not as the Biblical myth of creation described it. Each of these scientific discoveries did more than challenge established religious authority, they also dealt profound blows to human narcissism by weakening our pleasant sense of being special, distinct, and perhaps even omnipotent in the universe. Freud's work proved to be even more threatening to human self-esteem, so that while no educated person today holds to a geocentric theory of cosmography, or disputes the facts of evolution, many still feel free to dismiss Freud's fundamental discoveries as if they were merely unpopular hypotheses, rather than scientific truths derived from observation.

Freud's cynical and pessimistic comment about himself came as a result of his disappointment at the lack of interest on the part of the medical community of his day in regard to his findings about the importance of sexuality in the etiology of the neuroses. In actuality, the intellectual revolution Freud started goes far beyond his revisions of our understanding of neuroses, and of sexuality for that matter. What he did was to take up embryonic ideas about unconscious mental functioning that were just beginning to be studied in a serious way by the neurologists, psychologists, and psychiatrists of his day, and devise a totally innovative method of investigating them. This led to startling and troublesome new ways of regarding every aspect of our thought processes, and consequently of every dimension of human life that is affected by the way our minds work. What Freud discovered is that much of our behavior and thought is influenced in a very important way by ideas, images, and memories that exist in our minds outside of consciousness and inaccessible to it. Furthermore, he discovered, this unconscious material is so inaccessible precisely because it is not welcome in our conscious minds.

He demonstrated that all of us, without a single exception, have developed elaborate psychological measures, of which we are completely unaware, to insure that this unconscious layer of material stays hidden from us.

Having reluctantly accepted that the universe was not just created to be a setting for human dramas, and having even more reluctantly admitted that human beings are only one amongst many forms of animal life on this planet, there was now an even greater disillusionment to face. Far from having been specially chosen to rule the earth, we are not even in as much control of our own thoughts and activities as we have always believed ourselves to be. Our motivations and reactions, our judgments and behavior, and the institutions and customs to which these give rise, are influenced by aspects of our personal histories, and of the way our minds work, about which we have no direct knowledge, and of which we remain in ignorance even when we try to understand ourselves. This blow to our view of ourselves remains hard to absorb, although an ever increasing number of people have adjusted to its implications. Some people have reached the optimistic conclusion that systematic study of the unconscious mind and its effects can possibly lead to an increased mastery and control of our lives. This viewpoint has very slowly gained recognition and acceptance, and has softened somewhat the painful discomfort that Freud's revolutionary revisions of our self-image first produced.

Freud was born in modest circumstances on May 6, 1856, in Freiberg in Moravia, and moved with his family to Vienna at the age of four. He was from the beginning a brilliant student, and was regarded by his family and himself as destined for great achievements. He was attracted to science, decided to study medicine and physiology, and eventually found himself at home in the laboratory of the great physiologist, Ernst Brücke. He was content with his research work on the invertebrate nervous system, but after a few years he was advised for practical reasons to take up the clinical practice of medicine. The necessity to make a living drove him to the study and treatment of diseases of the nervous system, of which the foremost expert at that time was Professor J. M. Charcot at the Salpêtrière in Paris. Freud's clinical acuity had quickly gained him recognition in Vienna; as a result he was awarded an opportunity to go to France to study with the great master in 1885.

Freud returned to Vienna in 1886, deeply impressed by Charcot's researches into the nature and treatment of hysteria, but the Viennese medical establishment reacted to Freud's enthusiasm with skepticism, and soon excluded him. He retreated into his private practice, utilizing electrotherapy (which he soon realized was not effective), and also hypnosis as the basis for treating his hysterical patients. In the most complete autobiographical summary of his career (1925), Freud notes that he used hypnosis not only to remove symptoms by suggestion, in accordance with the accepted practice at that time, but also to inquire of his patients about the origins of their hysterical symptoms. In this activity he was utilizing impressions gained from the work of another famous Viennese physician, Dr. Josef Breuer, who some years earlier had conducted an unorthodox but successful treatment of a complex case of hysteria by inducing his patient to talk about her symptoms while in a deep hypnotic trance. To learn more about hypnosis, Freud again traveled to France in 1889, observing the pioneers, Ambroise Auguste Liebeault and Hippolyte Bernheim, at work in that field. At the time, Freud (1925) writes, he "received the profoundest impression of the possibility that there could be powerful mental processes which nevertheless remained hidden from the consciousness of men" (p. 17). Since hypnotic suggestion alone proved to be of limited benefit to patients, Freud combined his research interest and his desire to increase his therapeutic effectiveness, and decided to try to reproduce Breuer's success by using the new technique with his own cases. Freud's experience soon confirmed the value of this modified technique, and he then convinced Breuer to collaborate in joint publication. A preliminary paper in 1893 was followed in 1895 by the now famous monograph, *Studies on Hysteria*, in which what they referred to as the "cathartic method" was described. This is regarded today as the direct forerunner of psychoanalysis.

I interrupt this brief chronology of Freud's career to underline the fact that he was led to his great discoveries by chance and by circumstances, and not by intention. He had great intellectual gifts, his powers of scientific observation were developed in his early days as a researcher, and he came to the study of neuroses from the orientation of a neuroanatomist, neurophysiologist, and clinical neurologist, and not from that of a philosopher or psychologist. In addition, his strong personality also gave him the courage to pursue his findings with confidence and determination, despite the criticism of his professional colleagues.

The first of Freud's major discoveries was that the disturbances at the source of neurotic difficulties were invariably of a sexual nature. When he first reported it, Freud was as surprised as everyone else by this finding. Freud (1925) writes, "I was not prepared for this conclusion and my expectations played no part in it, for I had begun my investigation of neurotics quite unsuspectingly" (p. 24). Even Breuer was uncomfortable with this result of their work, and their collaboration was soon terminated. The rest of the medical establishment was even more dismissive of Freud's surprising conclusion. Freud refused to be discouraged, and he extended his investigations to other forms of neurosis, those that were at that time called neurasthenias. Not only did he learn that sexual disturbances are at the root of neurasthenic problems as well as hysteria, he began to map out correlations between specific varieties of sexual etiology and their corresponding symptom pictures.

He had begun to suspect that hypnosis itself was not the curative factor in treatment, but that it was the patient's relationship to the doctor who conducted the hypnotic treatments that was crucial to its success. On one occasion, a young woman he was treating awoke from her hypnotic trance and threw her arms about Freud's neck. "I was modest enough not to attribute the event to my own irresistible personal attraction," he writes, "and I felt I had now grasped the nature of the mysterious element that was at work behind hypnotism" (1925, p. 27). He became determined to abandon hypnotism, and he began to suggest to his patients that they would be able to recall the inaccessible material without being placed in a hypnotic trance, since Freud was by then convinced that the important determinants of neurosis rest in the unconscious stratum of the mind. Eventually, he stopped asking his patients to concentrate on recalling the forgotten explanations of their symptoms. Instead he urged them to allow their minds to roam freely, without any conscious direction at all, and to faithfully report in words everything that occurred to them, whether or not it seemed useful or even pertinent, and regardless of any feelings of embarrassment or of the other constraints that apply to social conversations. To aid his patients to relax and speak freely, Freud retained from hypnosis the custom of having them lie comfortably on a sofa, while he sat behind them, out of their field of vision, as they communicated their thoughts to him. This new method of communication was called "free association," but Freud correctly realized that what came to the surface of the patient's mind was not "free" in the sense of being random or unstructured at all, but was determined by what was at that moment active in the patient's unconscious mind. Informed observation of the patient's free associations allowed Freud to learn what was hidden there, and thus to explain the unconscious sources of the patient's symptoms.

By trial and error, Freud had discovered a method of studying the mind superior to anything that had gone before; with the refinements that will be described in later chapters, it continues to be the fundamental methodology of psychoanalytic investigation and treatment to the present day. It has produced unique data of extraordinary value, surpassing any other method of study of the way the mind works. There are many who regard the development of this technique as Freud's most important achievement. The explanatory theories that he, and his successors, devised to account for the data obtained by this psychoanalytic method have changed, and will continue to change. This process of change is similar to that taking place in other branches of science, as new observational data requiring changes in theory continue to be collected by observers.

As an illustration, his new technique almost immediately permitted Freud to improve in a fundamental way the theory of what causes neurotic afflictions. He discovered that the forgotten explanations for patients' symptoms were always things that caused great distress to those individuals. "It was impossible not to conclude that that was precisely why it had been forgotten—that is, why it had not remained conscious" (1925, p. 29). The free association method showed what hypnosis had not revealed—that it is extremely difficult to overcome the patient's desire not to become aware of the troublesome unconscious material. This caused Freud to coin the term *resistance* to describe the force within the patient that opposes remembering. Thus was born the theory of repression, in which Freud proposed that there is a balance of opposing forces in the mind. At last the nature and importance of the unconscious stratum could begin to be understood as never before. Freud could now start to account for the observation that ideas and memories that have been pushed to the unconscious and held there continue to have the power to influence the individual's thoughts, emotions, and behavior, although only in disguised ways, such as in the form of symptoms.

The free association method also permitted Freud to learn that dreams are psychological products that have meaning, and that these hidden meanings can be understood. By treating dream images as subjects for free association, Freud was led to the discovery of an entirely new form of thought structure. The confused or absurd account of the patient's manifest dream, that is to say, that which is first reported to the doctor, is only "a distorted, abbreviated, and misunderstood translation [of] latent dream-thoughts [that contain] the meaning of the dream" (1925, pp. 43–44). Freud's study of dreams helped him to understand and describe the peculiar logic of unconscious thought processes, which differs very much from the logical structure of ordinary conscious mental life. Every dream is like a complicated puzzle, in which the actors and events portrayed are often the disguised representations of other people, ideas, and actions, both past and present. Freud exercised his great ability for creative theorizing, and proposed a hypothetical model of the mental apparatus based upon these studies of the formation of dreams and symptoms. All of this was included in a monumental book, *The Interpretation of Dreams*, which was published in 1900. Freud always considered it to be his masterpiece, and it is still studied by students of psychoanalysis today, ninety years after it made its first appearance in print.

This extraordinary burst of intellectual creativity, which was eventually to earn for Freud the lasting fame for which he had naively yearned as a youth, took place in a few short years at the end of the last decade of the nineteenth century. It did not come easily, and his struggles with himself were perhaps as important as those he had with the medical establishment which at first refused to recognize the value of his work. In order to illustrate what he accomplished, and what he had to overcome to do it, I shall return to the subject of his discoveries about sexuality, which have proven to be the most difficult to accept and therefore the most controversial of all his findings, even to this very day. I mentioned earlier that Freud was surprised to learn from his patients that sexual experiences, either current ones or, in surprisingly many cases, things that were recalled by his neurotic patients as having happened to them in childhood, played a decisive role in creating their neurotic symptoms. The more cases Freud had an opportunity to study, the more convinced he became that experiences of seduction of one kind or another at the hands of older people, such as nurses and other caretakers, and often even their own parents, had had a disturbing effect on the development of those children who were to become sufferers from neuroses in adult life. He reached this conclusion because his patients told him so, at first under the influence of hypnosis, and later on, when he had changed his technique, in the course of reporting their free associations.

An unusual circumstance of history has enabled us to obtain a rare degree of understanding of these early stages in the development of Freud's theories. In part because he had become isolated from the leading medical circles of his day, and, we may well imagine, in part also for personal psychological reasons, Freud formed a very strong bond of friendship with another physician, Dr. Wilhelm Fliess of Berlin, with whom he carried on an active correspondence during the period 1887 to 1904. Since they shared certain areas of scientific interest, Freud was able to describe to his friend the details of his work and his theories, including his questions and his doubts. Their relationship was a complicated one, and it came to an end shortly after the period of the great initial discoveries that I am summarizing here. The chief significance of the correspondence with Fliess, so far as posterity is concerned, rests in the light it threw on the evolution of Freud's ideas. Freud was exceedingly private about his life and work, and seemed to take delight in the thought that he would be a difficult puzzle for future historians and biographers to understand. Freud's daughter, Anna, a noted psychoanalyst, who was also her father's companion and intellectual heir, permitted a selection of her father's letters and other writings to Fliess to be published (Bonaparte, Freud, and Kris, 1954), so that we have a record of this period in his investigations.

Among the extraordinary steps Freud took to understand the workings of the mind was a serious effort to analyze himself. He made use of his own dreams, and applied his technique of free association to them; in his famous book on dreams (1900) which I have mentioned, many of the examples he gives are of analyses of his own dreams. He admits these are not presented in full, as he wanted to keep a balance between his scientific purposes and his desire for personal privacy. Of course one cannot imagine that anyone, including Freud, can very thoroughly analyze himself or herself without the help of an objective outside observer who can detect the areas of protective self-deception, among other things. However, what Freud was able to accomplish in his self analysis enabled him to come to a truly fundamental discovery about the sexual life of childhood.

His correspondence with Fliess reveals his growing suspicion that actual sexual experiences in childhood, such as he was told about by so many patients, could not possibly have occurred as frequently as his data suggested. Yet his patients were convinced of the reality of the memories that they recovered, usually bringing them out only after much work had been done to conquer their resistances to recalling and describing the events. Freud tells of his doubts, his frustration, and of the concurrent problem he was having in his efforts to analyze himself. He realized that he was fighting to overcome his own resistances. At last, in a famous letter dated October 15, 1897, Freud announces the solution to the problem. He had at last been able to uncover in his own psychology unmistakable traces of his possessive childhood love for his mother, and of his corresponding jealousy of his father, a situation that he immediately named the *Oedipus complex*, borrowing the term from Sophocles' play, *Oedipus Rex*. Freud now came to understand that the sexual seductions of childhood that had been uncovered by his work with patients had not necessarily occurred exactly as described; instead these were vivid wishful fantasies, taking many different forms. These fantasies may involve such activities as looking, touching, smelling, and the infliction of pain, the eating and excretory functions, as well as ones involving the genital organs, a variety of sexual acts, ideas about pregnancy and childbirth, and the anatomical differences between men and women, among other aspects of the broadened perspective of what is now referred to as infantile sexuality.

Freud's work changed our understanding of what is meant by sexuality, as well as changing forever our beliefs about the ignorance and innocence of children in respect to sexual matters. The complex varieties of pathologically perverse sexual activities performed by disturbed adults had been familiar to physicians, officials, writers, and others long before Freud's time. Anthropological studies of a variety of cultures have led to the recognition that many forms of behavior in addition to copulation are a common part of the acceptable range of erotically pleasurable practices common among human beings. Freud's theory of libidinal development integrated these data with his clinical observations, and presented a coherent picture of how people's physical and psychological capacities for pleasure form a complicated developmental continuum. Many of the crucial steps in this sequence take place in early childhood. Furthermore, although the immaturity of the small child's mind limits its ability to understand such matters, and assures that it will form confused and incorrect fantasies about sexual activities and reproduction, all little children are intensely interested in those things. They are also capable of passionate love, jealousy, rivalry, and unrealistic ambition to an extent far greater than was acknowledged before Freud's researches revealed the true state of affairs.

Such sexual fantasies constitute an extremely important aspect of the psychological development of all children. Because of their troublesome nature, they are repressed, but under certain conditions they remain a potential source of future difficulty for susceptible individuals. These fantasies, and other contents of the unconscious strata of the mind, have the property of seeming quite real to the individual, even though they have been forced out of consciousness by repression. Thus was born the concept of *psychic reality*, as a way of speaking of this feature of unconscious fantasy life. The term refers to the fact that the human mind is unable to judge that these unconscious fantasies are not real, just as the images in dreams, however illogical, are usually experienced as quite real, at least until the dreamer awakens. Freud's patients were telling him the truth, but they were telling the truth about their own childhood mental lives, and not necessarily about the actual events that had taken place in those formative years.

Once on the right track, Freud's work progressed well again and he had soon compiled a radical reevaluation of childhood psychological development that took into account this greatly expanded interpretation of what constitutes sexuality, and of its significance in normal and pathological mental life. His revised and systematized findings were presented in what is perhaps his second most widely read work after *The Interpretation of Dreams*, the *Three Essays on Sexuality* (1905). I shall describe later how Freud's work went on until his death in 1939, and how his theories underwent further major revisions, both in respect to sexual development and its significance, and in respect to other important aspects of mental life. Still, in these few short years, Freud shook the world, and established himself as a true creative genius, even though the world hardly noticed that it had been shaken at first, and was inclined to dismiss him as a fool, or a madman, for quite some time after his revolutionary books first appeared in print.

Freud worked in relative isolation for more than ten years after he and Breuer ended their collaboration in 1896. Gradually a small circle of interested pupils gathered around him in Vienna. In 1906 came news that the Swiss psychiatrists Eugen Bleuler and Carl G. Jung, along with others, had become interested in Freud's technique and his ideas, to which he had by that time given the name psychoanalysis. Two years later, in 1908, the Swiss and Vienna groups met in Salzburg for an informal congress, and agreed to establish a journal of their own for the exchange of ideas. There was also continuing strong opposition to the new ideas, and probably as a result, the small group of people who pursued their psychoanalytic studies grew closer to one another; they began to speak of the psychoanalytic movement, a wording that suggests their sense of special purpose. In 1910 they formed a loose organization of local societies which they agreed to call the International Psycho-Analytic Association; it has continued in existence to the present day. By the mid-1920s there were, in addition to the original groups in Austria and Switzerland, active psychoanalytic groups in Hungary, Holland, Germany, Great Britain, and Moscow, as well as in India and the United States. However, it seems that no sooner had the young and enthusiastic body of interested psychoanalysts begun to take its first steps together than a disturbing tendency toward divisiveness made its appearance.

It is impossible to present an authoritative and objective explanation of why, almost from its beginnings, psychoanalysis has been troubled by intolerant rivalries that have led to bitter disputes, withdrawals from the parent organizations, and the formation of new, independent groups or schools of psychoanalytic thought. No doubt, a combination of personal factors and sincere differences in theoretical emphasis have both played a part. Just as psychoanalytic research was helping its practitioners to be aware as never before of the importance of universal tendencies toward ambition, rivalry, and competition that originate in childhood mental life, it seems that some of these same individuals were living out those very tendencies in their own professional lives. First Alfred Adler, then shortly afterward C. G. Jung, replaced their early admiration of Freud and his thinking with increasing criticism, personal hostility, and then the establishment of schools of their own, in which either some single aspect of Freud's thought was elevated to a place of primacy in the theory, or some crucial part of it was discarded, or both. It may be said that, true to Freud's prediction, throughout the later history of psychoanalytic controversies, in almost every case, those who chose to separate themselves from Freud and his adherents in order to establish a new school of psychoanalytic thought were objecting to the emphasis on infantile sexuality. They had a tendency, either explicitly or implicitly, to replace this emphasis with some other feature of mental life as the central focus. There has always been a temptation among some analysts to attribute those movements that have branched off from Freud's theories to the resistances at work in the minds of those individuals who were primarily responsible for the changes in theoretical emphasis. In other words, psychoanalysts often suspect that theoretical differences among themselves may be based less on objective data than on irrational factors masquerading as scientific disagreements. Of course this does not mean that all innovations and challenges to the established doctrine are to be disregarded. It is important in each case to decide whether there is some real value in the new proposals, but the job of evaluation is a difficult one.

This brings me to one of the most troublesome aspects of the scientific evaluation of psychoanalytic theories. Physicians, psychologists, and even philosophers and other thinkers who have neither conducted any analytic treatments, nor had any personal experience as subjects of psychoanalysis, have believed themselves to be capable of examining the various doctrines and findings of psychoanalysis and reaching opinions about their validity. Such individuals find it unacceptable, perhaps even insulting, to be told by psychoanalysts that they are not in a good enough position to make informed judgments about this field. In other branches of science or philosophy, an individual is not thought to be disqualified from making evaluations on similar grounds, because the ability to be objective about the data is usually assumed to be possible in most branches of natural science. In fact, things in other branches of science and thought are often not quite so simple as that, but in any case, the necessary objectivity cannot be assumed to be present in respect to weighing and considering psychoanalytic propositions and data. You will recall that Freud discovered very early in his work that what is buried in the unconscious human mind is buried for good reasons; it is troublesome, threatening, and out of step with the individual's ordinary, everyday, realistic commonsense views, cultural and moral values, and self-image. Furthermore, Freud taught us that each of us, including himself, strongly resists coming to understand what is in our own unconscious minds, and employs a repertoire of mental tricks, disguises, and defenses to stay in comfortable ignorance of it. We are completely unaware that we deceive ourselves in this way; on the contrary we are always convinced that our protective distortions are instead quite correct and realistic.

The dilemma is immediately apparent. Psychoanalysts have learned that it is a basic and inescapable fact of human nature not to be able to be objective about our own psychology. When we tell this to other scientists and thinkers who examine our findings, and explain that only through a personal experience of psychoanalysis and, preferably, some experience analyzing others as well, can they acquire the perspective needed to evaluate psychoanalytic propositions, they cannot easily believe we are correct. They understandably respond that, instead, we may be introducing a possible loss of objectivity into the matter by limiting the sources of valid criticism to those who are within the profession. How are we to convince them that the nature of this branch of knowledge is so specialized that with the strongest and best will, attitude, and intelligence in the world, it still cannot be adequately assessed except by those who have acquired the necessary experience? This is a problem with no obvious solution, one which has led to many awkward and even painful controversies both within and around the profession of psychoanalysis. This is no less true today than it was in the time of Freud. I was recently reminded that Freud had adopted for himself a favorite dictum of his early teacher, Charcot, "Theory is fine, but it does not change the facts." Still, it was Freud who taught us that the human mind does not always see and weigh the facts objectively; even great scientists are subject to wishful thinking, prejudice, and unwillingness to see what is plain to others, even while they are certain that they are merely looking realistically at the facts.

There are a few other trends in the early history of psychoanalysis that I would like to mention before I bring this first chapter to a close. The tendency to interpret their colleagues' scientific quarrels as being the products of those individuals' unconscious problems was only one manifestation of the early psychoanalysts' sometimes indiscriminate enthusiasm for applying their new perspective on the mind. One can easily imagine that these pioneer psychoanalysts were very excited by the discovery of this vast new region of the mind, the unconscious. It must have been as if they had come upon a powerful new instrument to decipher mysteries, a way of seeing and understanding hidden meanings in all areas of human endeavor that had not been known or even guessed at by prior generations. Wisemen, shamans, leaders, priests, philosophers, and scientists have tried for centuries to figure out the unknown; predicting the future, guessing the mystery of dreams, interpreting the significance of natural phenomena and the nature of the world beyond tangible measurement has been an interest of human beings throughout recorded history. The analysts' enthusiasm rode along on the energy of this timeless desire for mastery of the unknown, so perhaps we can forgive them their excesses. At any rate, a burst of interest in what has become known as applied analysis, which is the application of psychoanalytic insights to social and cultural phenomena, started with Freud, and has continued as an avocational interest of many analysts to the present time. Freud's restless imagination caused him to examine works of art and literature, mythology, biography, anthropology, and of related aspects of psychology, such as the formation and functioning of certain kinds of groups, in the light of the discoveries of psychoanalysis. Many other analysts since then have added studies of this kind to the literature. Some of them are thoughtful and ingenious, some are wild speculations, and there are many others of all gradations in between the extremes.

The application of psychoanalytic ideas, and eventually, the adaptation of the psychoanalytic method, to treating the emotional troubles of children and adolescents represented another major trend. Freud's daughter, Anna, was a pioneer in developing treatment methods for the analysis of children. One of those controversies of which I spoke earlier developed in this new area of psychoanalysis. It arose between Anna Freud and Melanie Klein; the latter based her technique on some significant differences in theoretical emphasis from those advanced by the Freuds. Klein placed proportionately much more stress on the nature and consequences of childhood aggression than had the Freuds, and she proposed a complex new conceptualization of the development of the mind during the first eighteen months of the infant's life, with which they did not agree. Klein was born in Hungary, studied psychoanalysis in Berlin, and then established herself in London, where the training center she founded still flourishes. Analysts influenced by her ideas practice, write, and teach in all the countries of the world today, working with adults as well as children. Unlike some of the divisions that arose among the early psychoanalysts, Kleinian thinkers and Freudians have continued to coexist within the International Psycho-Analytic Association, where they debate their differences vigorously, challenge one another's thinking, at times with passion, but on the whole in a healthy and respectful way. Other schools, shaped by the work of British thinkers such as D. W. Winnicott, Fairbairn, and others, who paid a great deal of attention to the lasting influence of the nature of the early relationships formed by the child with its mother, rather than to its struggle to learn how to deal with its own wishes, have also stayed within the established organizations of psychoanalysis. Such differences of opinion and emphasis have pressed thinkers on all sides of the questions in psychoanalysis to examine their data and their theories, and to revise them as new knowledge has permitted.

It should be noted that the founder of psychoanalysis, Sigmund Freud, although he came to the great discoveries that truly launched psychoanalytic science at about the age of forty, continued to develop his ideas for more than forty years after his breakthrough. He worked long hours despite being handicapped for many years by a serious malignancy of the jaw, for which he required much surgery. Freud consistently refused to take medication to relieve the pain, in order not to cloud his sensorium and thus dull his psychological sensitivity. Despite these problems he continued to psychoanalyze patients, to teach other psychoanalysts, and to write scientific articles and books. As he gathered data that suggested that his formulations might be inadequate or incorrect in one respect or another, he altered or refined his theories to take account of the new observations. One of the most remarkable achievements of his extraordinary career was to have the flexibility, honesty, humility, and courage to admit uncovering a major mistake in his theory, and to put forward a fundamental correction to his basic conception of neurosis, and of the organization of the mental apparatus, as he was approaching seventy years of age, or almost thirty years after his initial discoveries had taken place.

Chapter 2

Freud and His Successors: The Major Developmental Stages in the Evolution of Psychoanalytic Theory and Technique

Sander M. Abend, M.D.

Psychoanalysis is three different things: a method of treating emotional illnesses, a means of investigating mental functioning, and a body of theory about the structure of the mind and how it works. Of course these three meanings of the term are related to one another. I mention this because as I try to outline the main steps in the evolution of psychoanalytic theory, it may be helpful to remember that this same word, *psychoanalysis,* may refer sometimes to one, sometimes to another of these meanings.

In psychoanalysis, as in all sciences, a theory is an attempt to account for the available data in a coherent way. The more data we can explain, and the more complete, logical, consistent, and clear the explanation, the more satisfactory we find the theory. But in every field, there are usually some problems that are not explained well enough by current theories, and as new observations provide better data, weaknesses in the theories become evident. Consequently, scientists have to continually improve their theories in order to provide better explanations of the available facts. One of my own great pleasures in the study of psychoanalysis is following the evolution of the theories to try to see what were the problems that Freud and his successors encountered that forced them to modify their concepts in order to integrate the new data. This process also helps prepare me for the challenging job of deciding how well rival or alternative theories do at explaining what we observe in patients.

I will begin again with the early discoveries, outlined in the previous chapter. As we noted there, Freud came to his study of psychological phenomena from his background in medicine, physiology, and especially neurology. It was only natural that he thought in biological terms about the data he gathered from his observation of patients. He saw the activities of the mind as expressions of the functioning of the nervous system, and his efforts to explain them were based on his understanding of the nervous system. At a very early date (1895) he tried to construct a theoretical model of the way the brain might work that could account for what he was learning about neuroses. This tentative work, which he planned to call "Psychology for Neurologists," was never published in Freud's lifetime, for the very good reason that he was not satisfied with it. His ingenuity is undoubted, but it is clear that his effort was premature, and he was correct in deciding to put it aside. It is interesting that many researchers, even today, are trying to build theories to bridge the gap between psychological observations and the physiological processes that must underlie them. I think it is reasonable to say that we are still a long way from being able to do that successfully. At any rate, as Freud progressed in his work, he gradually came to realize that his wish to make a psychophysiological theory was not likely to be successful, and he turned to constructing explanatory models in purely psychological terms. However, he never lost sight of the fact that psychological events grow out of a biological substrate, and the evidence of that way of thinking is apparent in all of his theories, from every stage of his work. He also never gave up his belief that some day science will provide enough information to permit the successful integration of physical and psychological phenomena into one coherent theory. The influence of Freud's biological orientation is apparent in his first attempt to reconstruct the pathogenic process in neurosis. I will now paraphrase Freud's summary of the theory of repression, which is the most important aspect of his earliest psychoanalytic theory. Freud starts with an imaginary normal situation. Suppose, he says, an impulse arises in the subject's mind which is opposed by other powerful impulses or considerations. A mental conflict would surely arise, and we would therefore expect that the two dynamically opposed quantities, which he proposed to call the instinct and the resistance, would struggle with each other in full consciousness until, let us say, the resistance proved to be the stronger. The instinct* would be repudiated, and its charge of energy, which Freud named its "cathexis," would be withdrawn from it, reducing its power. Freud thinks of this as a model of a

*This word in English is not a very satisfactory translation of the original German word *trieb*, and today it is more likely to be translated instead as "the drive."

non-neurotic solution. However, he says, in a neurosis the conflict undergoes a different kind of outcome. At the first contact with the objectionable drive impulse, for reasons unknown, and by mechanisms unknown, the mind prevents the drive impulse from winning access to consciousness and from motor expression. The drive impulse stays or returns to the unconscious level of the mind, but without surrendering its charge of cathexis, so it is not weakened. Freud named this process "repression." He considers it a primary method of defense in the mind, comparable to flight responses, and a primitive antecedent of the evaluating and condemning kinds of normal judgment processes that develop later.

There are further consequences of this first act of repression. For one thing, the part of the mind that effects the repression, called by Freud the ego, must keep the troublesome impulse out of consciousness by means of a constant expenditure of energy, since it has not lost its original force. Even so, the repressed impulse, although remaining in the unconscious, is able to find a substitute pathway for discharge by some circuitous route. It is modified by the resistance, but not completely conquered, so this impulse comes to the surface in the form of a symptom. The symptom is a compromise between the original repressed impulse and the alteration produced by the resistance of the ego. Later on we will discuss a different, modern elaboration of the term *compromise formation*, but at this time in the development of theory Freud intends only to indicate that the symptom is a distorted and perhaps deflected version of the original drive impulse. This theory of repression became the key element of the theory of the neuroses. It transformed the conception of the task of therapy into that of uncovering repressions and then gradually replacing them by acts of mature judgment, which might lead either to accepting or to condemning the drive impulses that, because of neurosis, had previously been blocked from direct expression.

The drive impulses are thought of as psychological manifestations of physical desires, and the idea that there is some form of energy attached to them, and that energies are required to repress them, are clearly derived from physiological formulations. Similar considerations influenced Freud's great work on dreams. He discovered that all dreams give expression to some aspects of thoughts that were important on the day preceding the dream, but he concluded that the energy to construct a dream must come from a thought that includes a reference to some repressed wish. Because the state of sleep is physiologically different, the repressive energies are weakened although not absent. Thus a wish that is normally forbidden can be expressed, although there is enough repressive force still available to disguise it to some extent. The underlying thought structure of the dream, in ingenious fashion, represents the fulfillment of such wishes, and also, at the same time, expresses other, less forbidden thoughts from the previous day that signify important, unsettled concerns in the dreamer's mind. The similarities Freud saw between the way symptoms are formed and the way dreams are constructed helped to convince him that he was on the correct path to discovering the fundamental principles of the workings of the mind.

The surface of the dream can be regarded as a puzzle; a set of encoded thoughts, mostly expressed in the form of visual images. As I stated previously, through the free association method it became possible to decode these complicated puzzles and see the thoughts behind them. Those carried over from waking life Freud called the day-residues, which provide the materials from which the powerful repressed wishful thought constructs the dream. Freud called this process the dream work, in which the hidden, or latent, thoughts were converted into the manifest dream. It consists of a unique way of treating the thought material, so that component parts become condensed, a single image or element may stand for several ideas, and the psychological emphasis becomes displaced, which means that what is most important may be attached to images that appear to be trivial, and vice versa. These mental mechanisms are characteristic of the most primitive aspects of mind, and they persist in all aspects of unconscious thinking, not only in dream formation. The dream thoughts are first dramatized, then further disguised by the censorship activities that are also evidence of the remaining effects of repression. You can see that this concept of how the dream work goes on also assumes that there are psychic energies that can be detached from one image and put on another. Some dreams are unsuccessful in their efforts at disguising what is most troublesome to the subject, and these can be filled with anxiety, even to the point where the dreamer awakens in distress. Other dreams express physical needs like hunger or thirst rather directly, and some are so well disguised and defended that the psychoanalyst cannot help the patient to understand very much of what they convey. Take note of the almost physical conceptions like cathexis, repressive forces, strata of the mind, qualities of the mental apparatus, and so on in Freud's formulations. Nevertheless he made a new theoretical model of the way the mind works to explain dream formation, which was now expressed in terms of perception, memory, the fate of images, and other purely psychological concepts.

As for sexuality, I have already described something about Freud's first theoretical steps and how he arrived at them. In brief, he broadened the view of what is to be considered as part of the sexual function of humans. He outlined a development from the beginning of life, in which pleasure is attached to other vital functions, and to the physiological activities and parts of the body involved in them. He identified erotogenic zones; first the oral zone, since taking nourishment and its associated events is the earliest preoccupation of the infant, followed by the anal zone, since elimination and its control is the next major developmental step the child must master. This is followed in normal development by the increased importance of the genitalia as a source of pleasurable sensations. Little children, who enjoy being touched, held, and fondled by the adults who take care of them, gradually become aware that the genitalia are even more sensitive than the skin of other parts of the body, and this centers their attention on those areas. Children learn to touch themselves for pleasure and comfort, and by the time they do so they are also mentally capable of imagining scenes involving others, derived from their observations and fantasies about the sexual activities of their parents. Confused, inaccurate, and complicated as their childish ideas may be, these mental events involve jealousy and rivalry, and wishes to participate in the sexual and reproductive activities of the adults who are so important in their lives. This produces great conflict and distress as well as pleasure, since children misinterpret the physical acts of lovemaking and childbirth as physically harmful and dangerous, and because their intense wishes to love and be loved by one parent means that the child regards the other parent as a competitor who has to be eliminated. However, the child still also loves that other parent too, and does not wish to lose him or her, and besides the child now thinks he or she has good reason to fear punishment for these frightening rivalrous wishes. There, in brief, is the oedipal stage, or as Freud called it first, the phallic–oedipal stage. He believed that small children of both sexes do not understand the genital anatomy correctly, but mistakenly think that all people either possess a penis, or have somehow been damaged by losing it—are castrated, in other words. This belief persists in the unconscious mind even after the true facts are learned by the older child. Such unconscious fantasies become the source of much psychological confusion and distress in later life.

Because of the conflicts caused by these upsetting ideas connected to the pleasure-seeking sexual impulses, after a time children repress their childhood sexual wishes, and the masturbatory acts that accompany them, and enter a period of latency that lasts until the physiological changes of puberty reawaken sexual feelings and desires. I want to emphasize that this picture of psychological development in childhood is a strongly biological one, and rests on observations of children as well as on reconstructions from psychoanalytic data that Freud obtained from his adult patients. I should add that though everything I have just summarized is contained in Freud's earliest theoretical papers, even he had difficulty in fully accepting and believing the extent and importance of childhood sexual life and its associated conflicts. Although he knew the stages of sexual development are universal, he persisted in believing that a great difference exists between the impact of the associated sexual conflicts on those children who will become neurotic, compared with their effects upon the rest of us normal people. Present-day thinking emphasizes that even normal development is profoundly influenced by the consequences of these childhood stages and events. Freud also needed almost twenty-five years of further study to realize how much of significance actually takes place in the first years of childhood, since even he thought at first that many of the sexual ideas of early childhood only become psychologically important in puberty and afterwards. Furthermore, his formulations were not able to account for the differences in development between little girls and little boys, and in fact the careful study of female sexual development really did not begin until the 1920s, and aspects of it are still in dispute. It is not surprising, when you consider all these difficulties, that sexuality and its consequences became the most controversial of all the findings of Freud's psychoanalysis.

Freud continued to refine his formulations, and he eventually developed a topographical model of the mind, based on the idea that what was unconscious lies in one system, what is conscious lies in another, and that thoughts that are not conscious at the moment, but which are not blocked from becoming conscious by repressions, remain in a third system, called the preconscious. Freud used the word system to describe these parts of the mind because he meant to suggest more than the observable fact that their contents can be described as conscious or unconscious, but that they are each also organized in certain distinctive ways. I will not try to explain this very complex theory further, primarily because it was eventually replaced by another, more useful theoretical model of the mind that we will describe in later chapters. However, in the topographical theory emphasis was placed on the unconscious and the barriers between it and consciousness. Treatment was directed toward identifying the troublesome unconscious thoughts and bringing them into consciousness, but it was understood that in order to accomplish this successfully, the resistances that serve to block access must be done away with by psychoanalysis. Freud believed that repression, the prime mechanism of resistance, somehow produces a change in the nature of libido (sexual drive energy), turning it instead into a toxic product, anxiety. He thought that the successful undoing of repressions by psychoanalytic treatment could thus eliminate anxiety and other symptoms and permit more normal expressions of sexuality to take place. The balance of forces in the mind, based on the discovery of the Oedipus complex, were conceived of as comprising the instincts, or drives derived from sexuality, on the one hand, and self-preservative drives or motives, attributed to attunement to the requirements of the external world, on the other.

The empirical discovery of phenomena in the treatment situation that are collected under the important term *transference* led to the refinement of psychoanalytic technique in this middle stage of Freud's theoretical development. Transference means simply that childhood wishes, perceptions, and attitudes, originally formed in relation to the child's parents and other important figures of those early years, persist into adulthood in the unconscious mind, and become transferred, without the subject realizing it, onto the figure of the therapist. The most dramatic form of this phenomenon is when the patient forms a strong romantic attachment to the analyst, but many other expressions of transference occur. Freud noted that patients' wishes to be liked, favored, taught, approved of, and encouraged by the doctor are mild variants of libidinal transference attachments. Also, sensitivity to imagined criticism and resentments of other kinds, competition, even struggles to defeat, humiliate, and destroy the doctor may appear as transferences of a hostile kind. Freud understood that the appearance of such transferred wishes and attitudes are excellent opportunities to recognize important components of patients' unconscious minds, and are important clues to their repressed past. At the same time, transference expressions serve as resistances to analyzing the influence of the repressed unconscious. The patient experiences his or her transferences, whether loving or hostile, as real, and has no awareness that they come from the past. A strong wish to gain the analyst's love or approval, or a strong wish to combat the analyst, can temporarily overpower the patient's willingness to cooperate in the treatment by speaking freely about everything that enters his or her mind. Since the process of analysis is an attempt to recover the repressed past through speech, these transference attitudes can interfere either with remembering, or with telling the analyst certain uncomfortable thoughts, or both, and that is why they constitute resistances. Freud's genius, as he encountered and recognized these problems, enabled him to see that he could attack the repressions that cause neurosis by helping the patient to see and understand that the transference resistances are manifestations in the present of the childhood origins of the neurotic problems. The patient, if the treatment is successful, can come to experience in the relationship with the analyst, with great clarity and conviction, the patterns of his or her childhood relationships. Both the important wishes and the factors that caused them to be repressed in the first place are repeated in the patient's transference relationship to the analyst. Through gentle, objective, and noncritical observation, and repeated tactful interpretation to the patient of what the analyst sees in these patterns, the psychoanalytic process gradually enables the patient to gain more objectivity, to see that the transference reactions to the analyst are unrealistic, and to become convinced that these originate in the past. The barriers to remembering may be overcome, and the possibility to correct the immature and psychopathological ways of dealing with the drives that were instituted in childhood is provided by this special situation of psychoanalytic treatment.

Success or failure was thought to depend on many factors, including how well the patient could be persuaded to regard his or her transferences as irrational, and therefore be encouraged to look to the past for explanations of their nature. Before moving on, I must mention one other factor that Freud considered important in determining the success of psychoanalysis, because its subject matter has other important implications that came to play a role in theoretical controversies that emerged in later years. Freud believed that transferences repeat patterns of emotional relationships from the oedipal stage and afterwards. His opinion was that infants before the age of three or so, when the oedipal stage begins, are not yet maturationally ready to attach their libidinal drive energy to other people. From a psychological standpoint, the important persons in a child's life only achieve stable representation in the child's mind as the child develops past the earliest preoedipal stages. These mental images of significant people are called object representations, based on Freud's idea that they stand for the objects of the child's drive wishes. They only become charged with consistent psychological importance in the oedipal stage, and not before. In the preceding stages of development, Freud believed, the infant could only invest libidinal energies in its own body, self, or ego (Freud used different ways of saying this at different times). In other words, the young child is considered to be self-absorbed, or narcissistic in those preoedipal years. Freud developed some complicated formulations for how narcissistic libido changes into object libido, and how the reverse can happen as well. These are good examples of how the earlier levels of theory, while serving reasonably well for a time, eventually proved inadequate. For our present purpose, let me say that Freud believed that very disturbed individuals, such as psychotics, had not achieved the capability to form consistent object relationships, that is to say the investment of libido in their objects, rather than themselves. Such persons were thought not to develop true transferences, and therefore were not accessible for psychoanalytic treatment.

Freud had developed an effective empirical knowledge of how to carry out successful psychoanalytic treatment in suitable cases. He published a series of papers describing the principles of psychoanalytic therapy. These emphasized the importance of analyzing the patients' transference manifestations. The best way to do this, Freud discovered, was by adopting an attitude toward the patient that he compared to a surgeon's objectivity. He stressed encouraging the patient to free associate, while paying careful attention to everything that was said, as well as to whatever might interrupt these communications. The analyst was instructed to adopt a noncritical, nonjudgmental attitude toward everything the patient revealed, and try only to interpret, that is to say explain to the patient the psychological meaning of what came forward. The analyst was not to give any advice or instructions on how to conduct life, or to use his or her own life experiences as examples with which to try to influence or inspire patients. Psychoanalysis means exactly what it says—the analysis of the patterns of the patient's mind, explaining the nature of resistances, and of the hidden unconscious wishes and conflicts. When successful, this work could overcome repressions so that patients became able to remember certain especially important early childhood experiences, called traumas, that had contributed to distorting their psychological development. The undoing of repressions, the recovery of important memories, and the increased understanding of the unconscious mind that was thus gained by patients led to the relief of symptoms, and healthier development.

As Freud gained more and more clinical experience, he struggled to find ways to explain behaviors in patients that went against the idea that self-preservation is a prime motive in psychology. He had no fully satisfactory explanation that accounted for severe guilt reactions, self-defeating, self-punishing, and even self-destructive behavior.

He tried to understand severely depressed, melancholic patients by means of an ingenious formulation that included the concept of identification, in which the patients acted as if they unconsciously thought of themselves as identical with another individual who had been lost to them. Their excessive self-reproaches, symptoms of the melancholic state, were seen through psychoanalysis to be angry thoughts directed at the lost other person, whose representation had somehow become incorporated into the patient's own self. This complicated formulation, which I have not presented in full detail, used some clever and correct clinical observations, but it did not work well enough to integrate all the new data having to do with aggression and its consequences in human psychology. Furthermore, the more Freud studied resistances, the more he realized how complicated they can be. While repression remained a central feature of his understanding of them, he noticed and described other mental defenses that are used to alter the forbidden drives. He saw that these defenses are frequently partly or even fully unconscious, and that patients are usually not aware of the extent of their self-directed aggression, or of its significance, so that these, too, can often be described as unconscious.

In a series of interrelated steps Freud gradually modified his theories in a truly fundamental way. First he dropped the emphasis on self-preservative drives as the prime opponents of sexual drives. Instead he proposed that there are two inherent drives in human beings, one libidinal and the other aggressive. Each one's wishful expression can lead to conflict within the individual. Again, he thought these drives are rooted in the biology of the organism, but he tried to explain their consequences in purely psychological terms. He replaced his topographical theory of the mind, which emphasized unconscious, preconscious, and conscious systems, with a new model which has come to be called the structural theory. In it he proposes that we regard the activities of the mind as being arranged in groups of functions. To that group which lies closest to physical needs, and gives rise to the desires expressed in the drives, he gave the collective name, the *id*. Another set of functions that involve such things as control of motility, evaluation of reality, perception, thought, integration of mental functions, memory, judgment, defenses against drive expression, and so on, he thought of as constituting the *ego*, borrowing that term from a somewhat different earlier usage. A third set of functions that are concerned primarily with morality, that is, with the evaluation and consequences of issues of what is good and what is bad, was named the *superego*. These three "structures," which are not to be thought of as literally existing in reality, or as having actual physical locations in the brain, provide an excellent device or framework for explaining the observations of mental conflicts and their consequences.

The id is thought of as largely the more primitive, unconscious seat of the aggressive and sexual drives, and it is imagined to persist in a relatively unchanged state throughout the course of life. The ego constitutes all that can be directly observed; its functions are regulatory in the sense that it mediates between the demands of the id, the requirements of external reality, and the special requirements of the morally controlling superego. The ego begins to form and develop from birth; it reflects experience as well as maturational forces; becomes more complex as time goes on; and has the plasticity to adapt to changing circumstances, and to be influenced by psychoanalysis. The superego is thought to develop later in childhood. While the parents and other caretakers provide controls on the small child's behavior, and give it a sense of what is right and what is wrong, what is acceptable and what is forbidden, as the child passes through the oedipal stage it constructs its own internal ability to judge and control its wishes. This structure incorporates the parents' judgments, and also some imaginary ones that grow from the child's own theories about what is good and what is bad. The superego also provides ideals that direct behavior and influence the regulation of self-esteem. Its formation is a critical step in development because it permits the older child to be able to adapt its behavior to the world independent of direct and constant supervision from others.

This newly revised theory of the mind was described in an important paper, published in 1923, entitled "The Ego and the Id." Three years later, in 1926, Freud published another paper that completed the revolutionary changes he was making in his fundamental theories. In "Inhibition, Symptoms, and Anxiety," Freud made the remarkable announcement that he had been wrong all along about repression causing anxiety. Instead, he explained, it is the other way around. When threatening wishes from the id press toward expression in thought or action, they cause anxiety because the child believes these wishes would have dangerous consequences. A small amount of anxiety serves as a signal of danger, and causes the mind to activate repression and other defenses to block off the wish and avoid the danger. Just as with anxiety dreams, if the defenses are only partly successful, the patient may suffer greater degrees of anxiety, eventually at a conscious level; this is one type of symptom. Another result of the defenses could be the complete avoidance of activities that are connected with the forbidden wishes; this appears as an inhibition of one kind or another. There are also many other kinds of symptoms that express the wishes in forms altered by the defenses. Freud described a developmental series of imaginary danger situations that cause the child to mobilize defenses against the sexual and aggressive wishes it thinks are forbidden. These dangers correspond to the child's own stage of development, and they are, in order of appearance, (1) the loss of the important person, usually one parent or the other; (2) the loss of the important person's love for the child; (3) the loss of the penis, castration; and finally, (4) guilty self-reproaches. Anxiety in one form or another is connected with these dangers, which seem very real to the small child.

In 1926 Freud was seventy years old, and had been devoting all of his energy to psychoanalysis for over thirty years. It is truly amazing that this proud man could admit he had been so mistaken in his basic theory, and bring out corrections of such significance, at that point in his life. He continued to work at problems in psychoanalysis until his death thirteen years later, but his major contributions were now complete, and it remained for his successors to explore and develop the possibilities his theoretical discoveries had opened up for the understanding of human beings and the relief of psychological distress.

The profound impact that the new theory would have on the technique of psychoanalytic treatment required a number of years to be systematized. Freud's daughter, who had worked closely with her aging father, produced an important book, *The Ego and the Mechanisms of Defense* in 1936, in which these changes were described. It was now clear that the analyst observes verbal and behavioral data that are presented as a result of what can be described as the functioning of the ego, and makes inferences about the contributions to this material of elements derived from the id and the superego, as well as from the ego itself. In other words, behavior is now seen as the result of the interaction of forces from these three agencies of the mind. Analysis is particularly concerned with the effects of psychic conflict, and Anna Freud's book, and other later works, showed how the therapeutic emphasis had shifted to stress an understanding of the ways in which the various ego activities, and especially the ego's defensive abilities, altered the expression of forbidden unconscious drive wishes. Much more attention was paid to the moral influences of the superego, which can under some conditions become much too severe, so much so as to sometimes also mobilize defenses against their powerful impact. The new theory also made it easier to see that development not only is affected by specific experiences that have an overwhelming traumatic effect on the young child, but also by environmental forces of a more subtle and persistent nature, such as certain parental attitudes and behavior, whose traumatic influence is chronic rather than acute. To give simple examples of the latter type of trauma, it is easy to imagine that a child's psychological development will be affected in a number of ways if the child is raised in a home with a violent and unpredictable alcoholic parent, or one where a parent suffers from severe mental or physical illness. Exactly what the effects of such conditions would be depends on many other factors, and the psychoanalyst always tries to study the unique consequences of these and other forces on the way each patient has handled his or her important conflicts. It also became easier to say that psychic conflicts are a universal experience in childhood, and that their outcome influences much more than just the possibility of developing a neurosis later in life. Normal adaptations to life also reflect the way each individual has handled the Oedipus complex and the other instinctual conflicts of early life. Furthermore, many not so normal outcomes of development result, not in acute neurotic symptoms, but in pathological character traits, such as, for example, an exaggerated tendency toward rebellious and provocative behavior toward persons in authority. These behaviors, too, can be studied, explained, and treated by psychoanalysis.

In 1939, the prominent analyst–theoretician, Heinz Hartmann, published *Ego Psychology and the Problem of Adaptation*, in which he made explicit what had been gradually becoming clearer to psychoanalysts, namely, that psychoanalysis was more than a theory of neurosis, it had evolved into a general psychological theory of human development. It is least well adapted to clarifying the constitutional factors and other purely physical contributions to human development, although it assumes that these are always present and important. It is uniquely positioned to study the psychic and experiential factors that play a part in development because of its attention to their unconscious dimensions, and because of its respect for the effects of earlier experiences on later appearing aspects of personality and behavior.

During the decade of the 1930s, another trend appeared in addition to those I have just described. Other schools of psychoanalytic thought were emerging, and one theme that could be seen as gaining prominence was increased attention to the impact on later psychopathology of experiences in the very earliest period of childhood, the years before the oedipal stage of development. Greater concentration on examining the nature of the child's characteristic ways of relating to its earliest objects, that is, the mother and others who provide care, and in particular of observing more or less permanent consequences of the preoedipal developmental experiences, assumed greater importance for thinkers of these other schools. Eventually, these questions came to interest psychoanalysts of all schools of thought, including those of us who still consider ourselves most completely Freudian in our theoretical position.

One other factor that had consequences for the spread and growth of psychoanalysis during the 1930s and afterward was the sociological effect of the rise of Hitler and Nazism on the European intellectual community. Many psychoanalysts were Jewish, both in the early years of Freud's influence and later on. There were also many who were not Jewish, including some of the most influential thinkers in the field, but even the non-Jews tended to be anti-Nazi, either because they were political progressives or simply because of their humanistic, antitotalitarian attitudes. They rightly feared persecution from the Nazis, and as many as could do so emigrated from western Europe. Even Freud himself, ill and aged, left Vienna after the Anschluss (the takeover of Austria by the Nazis), moving to London in 1938. Large numbers of psychoanalysts moved to America, to Latin American countries, and to Britain. As a result, psychoanalytic development was enriched and stimulated in those places, and the science had to be reestablished in Europe after the conclusion of the war and the defeat of Nazi Germany.

In the years since the end of World War II, psychoanalysts have grown in numbers, and psychoanalytic thought has grown in influence everywhere. It is beyond the goal of this chapter to present a detailed history of this most recent period, but it will be discussed in subsequent chapters. However, I will mention some highlights. For analysts who considered themselves to be orthodox followers of Freud, the trend of the immediate prewar period continued, and interest in pursuing the advantages of the structural theory led them to concentrate on learning more about the ego, so much so that this branch of the psychoanalytic tree became known as ego psychology. This does not imply less interest in the instinctual drives or psychic conflict. The study of the effects of unconscious psychic conflict on human psychological functioning remained at the center of analytic thought, and the more they learned about it, the more complex its consequences were seen to be. In the early days of psychoanalysis, a neurosis was thought of as an aberration existing in a healthy personality. Its successful treatment was imagined to be similar in nature to the treatment of a specific physical illness; namely the restoration of the patient's health. The more modern view sees neurotic symptoms, character traits, and adaptations as related to one another; all are influenced by childhood development, and by the outcome of universal unconscious conflicts. Analytic treatments have grown longer, and now try to take more of the patient's psychology under examination. Technique has expanded to pay attention to more aspects of the patient's unconscious, including such things as his or her unconscious responses to the treatment situation itself, as well as to the personality and actions of the analyst. Instead of a sharp dividing line between the transference, which is thought of as an expression of the neurosis, and a more mature and realistic relationship to the analyst that could be regarded as separate from the distorting transferences, analysts have come to realize that the influence of the unconscious is even greater than had been suspected earlier. Every aspect of what takes place in psychoanalytic sessions, and even the most practical commonsense areas of the patient's observations, reactions, and communications, are now regarded as data to be examined psychoanalytically, so that the possible influence on them of unconscious predispositions can be detected, understood, and revealed to the patient through the analyst's interpretations. As patients progress in psychoanalytic treatment, they become better able to recognize their own unconscious patterns, and take greater responsibility for understanding themselves, so that the analyst's role is less that of an authority who tells the patient what things mean, and more that of a collaborator in a journey of self-exploration and self-understanding.

Controversies arise even among practitioners who are of the same school of psychoanalysis, and contending schools separated by more important differences of theory and technique have become more of a factor on the psychoanalytic scene during this most recent period of its development. These variations include the different ways of trying to understand the effects of the first two or three years of life upon later psychological development and problems. There are different views as to whether the analyst helps some patients, or even all patients, better if he or she more actively encourages changes in the patient, rather than following the traditional Freudian role of limiting the therapeutic influence to the objective interpretation of resistances, unconscious wishes, and other components of conflict. There are different opinions about which aspects of conflict are more significant, and even about whether the modern psychoanalyst should pay attention to other factors in psychological development in addition to or instead of unconscious conflict.

Freud is the common ancestor of all psychoanalysts, but by now enough generations have passed so that, as in biology, the various children and grandchildren of this common ancestor can, in some cases at least, barely be recognized as belonging to the same family. Many people today call themselves psychoanalysts, and consider the treatments they perform to be psychoanalysis, but their ideas and their training may vary so much that an outside observer could easily see that they do very different things, based on often incompatible beliefs. This is confusing for the public, and for students of human psychology.

All of the contributors to this book share a common point of view and emphasis in our view of psychoanalysis. We think of ourselves as, so to say, direct descendants of Freud; we are part of the traditional group that believes childhood unconscious instinctual conflicts of a sexual and aggressive nature have lasting and central importance in human development, and that a study of their influence, particularly through the transference that develops in a properly conducted psychoanalysis, leads to explanations of and improvements in patients' emotional suffering. We all find the structural theory to be the most useful way to organize the data, and we have been strongly influenced by those psychoanalytic thinkers and teachers, after Freud himself, who called themselves ego psychologists. We would probably disagree among ourselves about some aspects of psychoanalysis, just as any group of physicians might differ about the diagnosis of a particular patient's condition, or about some detail of the treatment approach to be recommended.

I cannot end my short review of the history of psychoanalysis without returning to the subject of biology, the soil from which Freud's earliest ideas about psychoanalysis grew. In recent years, advances in biochemical research have given rise to an entirely new approach to the treatment of mental illnesses. Originally confined to the treatment of psychoses, psychopharmacology has been advancing rapidly and extending its influence to the treatment of an increasingly wide spectrum of psychological disturbances. Psychoanalysts are just beginning to explore the possibilities and the complications of combining psychoanalytic treatments with medications, at least for some difficult patients. Careful research has not yet been carried out, and we can only imagine what the future will bring in the way of further advances and knowledge.

Chapter 3

The Role of Psychic Conflict in Mental Life

Charles Brenner, M.D.

The idea of conflict within the mind, of intrapsychic conflict, has been important in psychoanalytic psychopathology from the beginning of its development. I say "from" because it has retained its importance to the present time.

Today, on the basis of data now available to us, it is apparent that conflict is not limited to psychopathology. On the contrary, psychic conflict is as much a feature of normal mental life as it is of mental illness. The events of childhood inevitably generate significant psychic conflicts, ones that are as important to normal as to pathological development and later functioning. The fears and miseries of early childhood, the anxiety and depressive affect associated with the instinctual wishes of that period of life, leave an indelible mark on every one of us. It is not that

This chapter was presented as a lecture that was part of a colloquium offered by the Extension Division of the New York Psychoanalytic Society for Mental Health Professionals of the New York Metropolitan area.

childhood is all conflict and misery, there are plenty of joys in childhood too, but it is never as joyous as most of us like to tell ourselves it was for us. The conflicts of childhood determine those of all of adult life. The anxieties of adult life and its depressive moods and affects are the consequences, the echoes, of those in early childhood.

I think it will be best to begin by defining or describing what *psychic conflict* is, as the term is used by psychoanalysts today. What are the components of conflict and how do they interact in what we call conflict?

The first element of every conflict is a drive derivative, a childhood instinctual wish. By this is meant a wish for pleasurable gratification of a libidinal or aggressive kind. Since every such childhood wish contains both libidinal and aggressive elements, it is easy to put them together and say simply a wish for sexual gratification, where sexual implies both libidinal and aggressive. A common wish of this sort from the oedipal period is a wish to have a parent as husband or wife and to be rid of one's adult rival. Bear in mind that such a wish concerns a particular mommy and daddy; not any parents, but each child's own parents. Every drive derivative, in other words, concerns specific characters in each child's life. Each derivative is unique and different in one or another important respect from any other child's derivative. When we survey our experience with many patients, we can see important similarities, to be sure, important and far reaching enough so that we classify a drive derivative like the one just referred to as a positive oedipal wish. Nonetheless, when one is working with a patient, what one observes is a unique phenomenon, specific to that patient. It is not only specific as far as the people, the dramatis personae, are concerned. It is just as specific with respect to other details: parts of the body to be stimulated, for instance, or what one wants to do to the particular parent, and just how babies are made, and so on. The concept of drive is a generalization that is based on a survey of the wishes of many individuals, wishes observed with the help of the psychoanalytic method. A drive derivative is one person's wish or wishes, also observed by the method of psychoanalysis.

Libidinal gratification is intimately connected with certain parts and activities of the body, chiefly with what Freud called the erogenous zones. Aggressive gratification is less closely associated with those zones. What Freud rightly emphasized about the sexual wishes of children is that they include not only what we classify as sexually normal in adult life, but also what is included under the heading of sexually perverse. Childhood sexuality is polymorphous. The erogenous zones include mouth and anus as well as the genital organs. Sexual behavior and sexual wishes include looking, listening, smelling, sucking, defecating, and so on. Likewise, wishes to hurt, to injure, to get revenge, as well as wishes to be injured and to suffer, are part of the sexual wishes of childhood. The whole range of sadomasochism in sexual life has its origins in the wishes of early childhood and the conflicts to which they give rise.

To return to our main subject, conflict, the first component of conflict is a wish, partly libidinal and partly aggressive, for pleasurable gratification. What we know both from analysis and from direct observation suggests that in the first eighteen months of life the leading erogenous zone is the oral one. At about the age of eighteen months anal wishes become prominent, and at the age of three-and-a-half years wishes for pleasurable genital stimulation take their place in mental life as well. It is important to remember that although we speak of the oral, the anal, and the genital phases of childhood sexual development, oral wishes do not disappear after the age of eighteen months any more than the anal ones or the oral ones become unimportant after the age of three-and-a-half years. Once they have appeared, wishes connected with the various erogenous zones remain important throughout the rest of one's life. Wishes for pleasurable stimulation of oral and anal zones continue to be very important in the mental lives of four- and five-year-olds, and evidences of this are prominent in the conflicts of adult patients as well. Oral or anal fantasies are not necessarily signs of trauma that occurred in the first two years of life.

Freud assumed that everyone's mind functions according to what he called the pleasure principle. We are all trying to get as much pleasurable gratification as we can from infancy on, whether the gratification is oral, anal, genital, or whatever. Man is basically a pleasure seeking animal, as many before Freud have repeatedly remarked. How then can the desire for gratification of drive derivatives give rise to conflict?

The answer is that wishes for pleasurable gratification inevitably give rise to unpleasure in childhood as well. The mind functions not only to achieve pleasure. It is guided as well by an imperative need to avoid unpleasure. Man is as truly pain avoiding as pleasure seeking. Every child is for many years after birth dependent on its parents not only for physical care and protection but for pleasurable physical gratification and emotional gratification as well. Every child's sexual wishes necessarily bring it into troubles that in the last analysis arise from the fact that children are physically so immature for so many years and are so dependent physically and emotionally on the parents and other older persons in their environment. It is not only that a child's wish to get rid of one parent so that it can possess the other stirs up fears of reprisal. The child's physical immaturity makes the gratification of many of its wishes impossible under any circumstances, a fact that gives rise to as much unhappiness in childhood as it would and often does in adult life. Rivalry is not the only reason why derivatives give rise to unpleasure in childhood. Another is that the sexual wishes of childhood, especially those of the oedipal period, are impossible to gratify fully because of the immaturity of the child's sexual apparatus. Psychologically a five-year-old is sexually mature; physically a five-year-old must wait what seems to it forever before it can gratify its wishes. These experiences of the limits of one's body are, not infrequently, remembered as humiliations and defeats.

The unpleasure associated with childhood drive derivatives is what gives rise to or, more precisely, what triggers conflict in mental life. It is the second component of psychic conflict and it can be conveniently classified under two headings: the first is the familiar one of anxiety; the second is the less familiar one of depressive affect. What is the difference between the two?

Every affect is a composite of a sensation of pleasure or unpleasure and ideas. Anxiety and depressive affect are no exceptions. In each there is a sensation of unpleasure, a sensation that may be more or less intense. In the case of anxiety, if the unpleasure is intense, one speaks of panic or terror. If the unpleasure is very mild, one speaks of worry or unease. In the case of depressive affect, if the unpleasure is intense, one speaks of misery or of severe depression; if it is mild, of unhappiness or of slight sadness. As for the ideas, those that are part of any form of anxiety always have to do with danger, with some calamity that impends or threatens. Those that are part of depressive affect have to do with a calamity that is current, that is a part of life. To take a simple example, a child who fears parental disapproval or reprisal in connection with some drive derivative is, by definition, experiencing anxiety, whether mild, medium, or intense. A child who feels unloved or punished in connection with some drive derivative is again, by definition, experiencing some variety of depressive affect. Obviously the two are not mutually exclusive. On the contrary, they are closely related, so closely that they may at times be virtually indistinguishable. More often, though, they are easily separable and it is important clinically to make the separation.

In "Inhibitions, Symptoms and Anxiety" (Freud, 1926) Freud listed four calamities as the ideational content of childhood anxiety. In order of appearance they are object loss, loss of love, castration, and punishment. The time of appearance of each calamity seems to correspond roughly to the phases of libidinal development outlined earlier. Object loss, the earliest, appears sometime in the first eighteen months of life, loss of love more or less in the eighteen months following, and castration and fear of punishment during the genital or oedipal period from about three-and-a-half years to six years of age. What is of particular importance to keep in mind, however, is that, once it has appeared, each of these calamities continues to be important throughout the rest of one's life. Object loss and loss of love are calamities in the minds of five-year-olds as well as in the minds of much younger children. They are not necessarily pregenital in origin. All four calamities play major roles in mental life and all four become inextricably intertwined. A girl of five who feels castrated because she is not a boy is miserable in part because to her castration means being unloved as she wishes to be loved by father, just as her castrated state may in her imagination be attributed to mother's punishment for her rivalrous and murderous jealousy of mother. In the same way, a boy of the same age may fear loss of father's love not only for its own sake but as much or more because in his imagination it means father will punish and castrate him.

To repeat, then, the second component of psychic conflict, the component that acts as a trigger, is unpleasure in the form of anxiety, depressive affect, or both. Anxiety is defined as unpleasure with the ideational content that a calamity impends. Depressive affect is defined as unpleasure with the ideational content that a calamity has happened, that it is a fact of life. In either case the calamity is either object loss, loss of love, castration, or punishment, all eventually inextricably intertwined.

The third component of conflict is defense. Whenever either anxiety, depressive affect, or both appear in connection with a drive derivative, the mind responds in such a way as to reduce or eliminate unpleasure. Every such response, every effort to reduce or eliminate unpleasure, is what is called defense.

The traditional way to conceptualize defense is in terms of mental mechanisms. The term *defense mechanism* was popularized by Anna Freud (1936) in *The Ego and the Mechanisms of Defense*. Despite its popularity and its long and honorable history, however, I believe the term and the concept *defense mechanism* are misleading.

The traditional discussion of defense begins with a list of defense mechanisms: repression, reaction formation, regression, denial, projection, identification, reversal into the opposite, turning active into passive or passive into active, isolation, identification with the aggressor, and perhaps one or two more such as altruistic surrender and seduction of the aggressor. The list implies, and is generally taken to mean, that each of these mental operations is characteristically if not exclusively defensive. "Repression is a defense mechanism," means, "Repression = defense; repression is a mental mechanism that is used only for defense." In fact, however, this is not so. Any of the mental operations or mechanisms in the list is used at times for defense and at times for something else; for example, to further gratification of a drive derivative. None of them is exclusively used in the service of defense. They are not defense mechanisms in that sense.

Just as important is the fact that defense is not limited to any such list of mental mechanisms. Anything that will diminish or eliminate unpleasure is a defense, and that includes whatever the mind is capable of. Any and every capacity of the mind is, at times, used defensively. No mental functions are reserved for defense alone. Defense is not a short list of mental mechanisms.

So it is much better to avoid thinking of defense in terms of a few mental mechanisms and to keep in mind that whatever an individual does or thinks that serves the purpose of reducing unpleasure, whether efficiently or not, deserves the adjective defensive.

The fourth component of conflict is the superego, the aspect of mental functioning that has to do with morality, with ideas of what is right and what is wrong in the moral sense of those words. There is some difference of opinion about what to call superego in the first few years of life, but there is general agreement that the major share of its development as an agency of the mind takes place toward the end of the oedipal phase of development, say, in the sixth and seventh years of life, and that further development takes place during the rest of childhood and adolescence. Freud (1924) called the superego the heir of the Oedipus complex.

I myself think that term is too exclusive. There are too many important consequences of the Oedipus complex to justify singling out the superego as its sole heir. That it is, in the main, one of the important consequences of the oedipal phase is, however, unquestionably the case. In order to understand its development one must put oneself in the place of a five- or six-year-old.

To a child of that age what is morally right is what will please one's parents, what will win their approval. What is morally wrong is what will displease them, what will incur their wrath and disapproval. For a five- or six-year-old child its parents are conceived of as very powerful, if not omnipotent, and are the supreme arbiters. What they say is right *is* right. What they say is wrong *is* wrong. And, I should add, they need not literally say it. What counts is what the child is convinced they would say or have said, whether the child's conviction is based on fact or on fantasy. When a child is convinced that one or another of its drive derivatives will lead to parental disapproval in the form of banishment, loss of love, or castration, unpleasure appears in the form of anxiety. When a child is convinced that parental disapproval and retribution have already resulted from one or another of the child's drive derivatives, unpleasure appears in the form of depressive affect. The expectation of parental disapproval is what constitutes that aspect of superego functioning that Freud called fear of punishment. When this happens a defense is instituted. The child tries not to want to do what it thinks would offend its parent or, in the case of depressive affect, what it is convinced has offended its parent. The superego in such cases participates in conflict on the side of defense. So much so that in his first discussion of the superego Freud (1923) attributed the function of defense to the superego rather than to the ego, an attribution that he soon withdrew.

Superego functioning encompasses more than defense against a morally objectionable wish, however. Contrition, atonement, and identification with one's parents' moral attitudes, real or only imagined, are also ways of winning parental approval and, for that reason, aspects of superego functioning. The single word *guilt* is inadequate to characterize the affects stirred up by moral transgression. Self-punishment and self-injury as ways of winning one's parents' approval are universal aspects of superego functioning. One can often observe this very easily in the moral codes of behavior of social groups. Practicing Jews and Moslems, for example, believed that their spiritual father, whom they called god, would love them and not punish them if their penises were mutilated by circumcision, a custom whose origins were millennia earlier than the lifetime of whoever the biblical Abraham may have been. And other examples are legion.

Psychoanalytic observation often demonstrates that morally motivated self-injury and self-punishment are the result of unconscious impulses to visit on oneself the very calamities that I have just described as the ideational content of the anxiety and depressive affect that trigger conflict. For this reason, self-injuring and self-destructive trends instituted to win moral approval may themselves be defended against, as is the case with drive derivatives that arouse intense unpleasure. Instead of being on the side of defense, in such cases the superego is defended against. One is faced with an example of what Freud called an unconscious sense of guilt, of a need to punish or injure oneself that is defended against by repression or in some other ways. Everyone with psychoanalytic clinical experience is familiar with cases in which a patient arranges to fail, or to be injured, without being in the least aware that the suffering is something that the person does to her- or himself. So the superego participates in conflict in more than one way. It participates on the side of defense at some times, and it is defended against, it is the target of one's defensive efforts at other times.

Drive derivative, unpleasure in the form of anxiety or depressive affect, defense, and superego manifestations, these are the components of psychic conflict. What are its consequences, both normal and pathological?

What results from psychic conflict is a complexly determined mental phenomenon that one can conveniently refer to as a *compromise formation*. This is a term that Freud introduced long ago to describe neurotic symptoms. When he began to develop and use the psychoanalytic method he soon discovered that obsessional, hysterical, and phobic symptoms are compromise formations among a childhood sexual wish, moral strictures against satisfying the wish, and efforts to ward it off in one way or another. Our current ideas of compromise formation are clearly based on Freud's early formulation. Every compromise formation is a composite of drive derivative, anxiety, depressive affect, defense, and superego functioning. Every neurotic symptom, every neurotic character trait allows for some drive gratification, exhibits some trace of unpleasure, functions defensively, and expresses some moral injunction. A simple example will illustrate this statement.

A young adult, living with his parents, had to check the gas jets on the kitchen stove every time he left the house. When asked about this behavior, which he felt as an imposition he could not avoid, as something he had to do even though he would prefer not to do it, he told a fantasy he frequently had. It was that he left the house unaware that a jet was burning and that in his absence the house caught fire and burned to the ground. His father then had become so overwhelmed by the disaster that he suffered a heart attack and died, in the patient's fantasy, and the patient and the mother had to struggle along as best they could in poverty.

What I have just told you is what I mean by a compromise formation. In this case it was certain behavior that we call a compulsive ritual and accompanying fantasy. We assume that it is the result of a psychic conflict of which the patient himself had little or no knowledge. What does the compromise formation tell us about the conflict that underlies it? Or, better, what can we infer about the underlying conflict on the basis of what the patient has told us about his symptom and his association to it, i.e., the fantasy?

What about drive derivatives? Judging from the fantasy one has little hesitation in concluding that the patient wished to possess his mother, to have her to himself, and to be rid of his father. Judging from his ritual, one has as little hesitation in concluding that the patient expects very bad things to happen if he gives in to the drive derivative just referred to. He must not let those gas jets burn or a calamity will result. So his drive derivative causes anxiety. How about depressive affect? In his fantasy, misery results from the achievement of his unconsciously desired goal.

As for defense, there are several, as is nearly always the case. Analytic work over a period of many months made clear that the patient's childhood wish was to possess his mother sexually. Of this the patient was quite unaware when he first told about his symptom and the fantasy associated with it. His sexual fantasies were repressed, as were his castration fantasies. We can guess at them, but he could not. In addition the patient consciously wished only to save his home from destruction. There was excessive worry and a wish to do good instead of bad. The patient was equally unaware of any desire to kill his father. It was a heart attack that killed him, not anything for which the patient was directly or personally responsible. Nor was there any feeling of triumph at having his mother to himself. In his fantasy, it was the opposite, misery instead of joy.

Finally, superego manifestations are evident both in the poverty he imposed on himself in his fantasy as a consequence of his bad wishes, and in the compulsive feeling that it was his duty to make sure that no gas jet was burning in his absence from home.

As one can see from this example, in a compromise formation the drive derivative involved is gratified in a disguised and incomplete way, but still some degree of gratification of the drive derivative is achieved, even in a neurotic symptom. Anxiety and depressive affect are eliminated as much as possible. As long as he carried out his ritual, the patient was fairly comfortable. Not entirely so, but much more so than if he had been consciously aware of just what he really wanted to do. The defense distorted and limited the gratification of the drive derivative, and saw to it that unpleasure was kept in check. And superego manifestations played their part as well.

When is a compromise formation normal and when is it pathological? When is it a neurotic symptom or character trait and when is it an aspect of mental functioning that deserves to be called normal?

The answer to this question is not an easy one. I think, though, that we are in a position to answer it to the following extent. A compromise formation is to be considered normal if: it allows a sufficient degree of pleasurable gratification to a drive derivative; the accompanying anxiety and depressive affect are not too great; the inhibition of function resulting from the individual's defensive efforts is not too extreme; there is not too much in the way of self-punishment and self-injury; and one is not brought into too great conflict with one's environment, by which is meant principally the people with whom one is in contact in one's life. The compromise formation deserves to be labeled pathological if, on the contrary, there is not enough pleasurable gratification; if there is too much unpleasure; too much inhibition of function; too much self-injury/self-punishment; or if there is too great friction with the environment.

Implicit in what I have said about compromise formations thus far is something I wish to make explicit at this point. Everything that is conscious in our mental lives, everything of substantial importance and interest to us that we can observe about the mental functioning of others, is a compromise formation that is the result of conflicts that originated in childhood, triggered by unpleasure aroused in connection with drive derivatives. Normal and pathological compromise formations make up all of mental life that we rate as significant.

No psychoanalyst doubts the significance of compromise formation in psychogenic illness. All of us who treat mentally ill patients with psychoanalytically oriented psychotherapy or with analysis proper are more or less clearly aware of the fact that the symptoms and character traits of which our patients complain are compromise formations arising from psychic conflicts whose origins are in the instinctual life of childhood. I expect less unanimous agreement in reaction to the assertion that all of normal mental life that amounts to anything is also composed of compromise formations arising from childhood instinctual wishes.

I think one reason for this is that the psychoanalytic method is less used and less usable for the study of normal mental phenomena than for the study of mental phenomena that are pathological. No one is going to lie on a couch for fifty minutes five times a week and say everything that comes to mind to a stranger without having a very good reason for doing so. So far as we know, the only reason important enough is neurotic suffering and the hope of relief or cure. What makes it possible to use the psychoanalytic method at all to study normal mental phenomena is the fact that many aspects of the mental lives of our neurotic patients are normal, and that in the course of analysis one has a chance at times to learn more than one otherwise could about such normal phenomena. Freud himself went as far as the study of dreams and of slips and errors, both normal phenomena, but ones that even he regarded as on a sort of borderline between normal and pathological. That was why he called slips and errors examples of everyday psychopathology, examples of the psychopathology of everyday life. One can go some steps farther, I think, as I shall try to illustrate.

A forty-year-old obstetrician was the oldest of six siblings. Like himself, all his brothers and sisters were born in the farmhouse where the patient spent his childhood. Each delivery was a major event about which he was intensely curious, but which he was never permitted to witness, though witnessing animal births was a commonplace experience from his earliest years.

Thus the patient's choice of vocation, a normal aspect of mental functioning, gratified his wish, originating in childhood, to watch his mother give birth. It also gratified his childhood wish to be superior to his father, who was always deferential to the physician who attended the patient's mother during her many confinements, and was eager to help him during the delivery. It was also related to the anxiety and depressive affect associated with his childhood drive derivatives. As an obstetrician he felt competent and self-confident whenever a new baby was born, not insignificant and helpless, as he had felt when he was a boy.

His choice of vocation involved defense against childhood wishes also. None of the women he watched while they were in labor was actually his mother, and none of their husbands, who deferred to him, was really his father. Jealous and murderous wishes of childhood were held in check by the kindness and helpfulness he showed his patients. In brief, his vocational choice was exactly the sort of compromise formation, composed in the same way as the obsessional symptom of the young man whom I described earlier who had to check the gas jets whenever he went out.

Chapter 4

Applications of the Theory of Conflict and Compromise Formation to Clinical Phenomena: Narcissism, Masochism, Sadism, and Transference

Arnold Rothstein, M.D.

In this chapter a number of fundamental psychoanalytic terms and concepts are explored from the theoretical perspective of conflict and compromise formation.

Aspects of this chapter have been published in *The Journal of the American Psychoanalytic Association*, 39:363–375, and in *The International Journal of Psycho-Analysis*, 72:313–323.

In the previous chapter a model is described in which the mind is conceived as being interminably in conflict. The consequences of the conflicts are compromises between the four conscious and/or unconscious elements of conflicts resulting in fantasies and/or derivative enactments.

As noted earlier, the elements in psychic conflict are wishes for sexual gratifications, which give rise to unpleasure in the form of anxiety and/or depressive affect, which triggers the third element of conflict, defense. Defense reflects the mind's effort to reduce unpleasure. The fourth element in psychic conflict is the superego, by which ideas of what is right or wrong in the moral sense is stressed.

From this perspective all mental phenomena, whether normal or pathological, can be thought of as compromise formations. Compromise is conceived of as a central organizing tendency of the mind.

SADOMASOCHISM

Freud (1905) considered masochism descriptively as pleasure in physical pain and/or in the pain associated with experiences of humiliation or subjugation. In this chapter, sadomasochistic phenomena are conceived of theoretically as deriving from conscious and/or unconscious fantasies. This perspective emphasizes the dynamic point of view while deemphasizing certain descriptive designations and some of their diagnostic implications.

Now analytic data will be presented from a case in which the pathologic compromise formations that underlie the patient's masochism contribute to its expression in neurotic symptoms, character traits, and perverse enactments.

For the purpose of this presentation data will be presented that stress its expression in neurotic symptomatology.

Mr. X. is a thirty-four-year-old successful lawyer; he is married. Psychic pain was prominent in his symptomatology. He began the first session of a week in the fifth year of his analysis by reporting in an agitated manner some humiliating aspects of a weekend event. On this day his discomfort was more acute than was usual for him. The psychic pain in his agitation was particularly impressive to me. I understood his agitation to reflect an intense experience of anxiety and depressive affect related to his fantasies of both fearing humiliation and feeling humiliated.

Mr. X. began his session by reporting:

> I was called by my uncle's wife at 10 P.M. on Saturday night and told he had been arrested and was being held by the police. I told her I would go to the police station and get him released. On the way there I became obsessed with the idea that everyone at the precinct would think my uncle was my homosexual lover. I know that has to do with you (that is, the analyst). When I arrived at the police station it became clear to everyone that I was a person of influence with the power to make them uncomfortable. They were very courteous and I was able to get my uncle released on bail without any difficulty. While I was there I had to let them all know I was married. I was terrified they'd think I was homosexual.

In response to his conscious masochistic fantasy of anticipating feeling humiliatingly embarrassed, my ensuing interpretation emphasized a defensive aspect of the compromise formation. I commented, "You felt quite potent in the way you were able to help your uncle." Mr. X. said "yes" and was silent for a while. I interpreted, "Your painful fantasy helped you diminish the frightening feeling that you were quite a powerful man."

Despite the fact that Mr. X. is a highly respected professional and an excellent athlete, he has characteristically been unable to experience and report satisfaction and pride in his accomplishments at work or in sports. However, in response to the interpretation, he spent the next twenty minutes freely describing his joy in his skills at work and at play. With glee he said, "I'm good at a lot of things." After a moment I responded, "You're enjoying feeling potent at work." He agreed. His associations shifted to a friend whose competitive wishes prevented him from acknowledging Mr. X.'s skills. Mr. X. stated, "The son of a bitch couldn't acknowledge what a good lawyer I am. I literally wanted to blow him away." His associations shifted to his lifelong experience of his father as often indifferent and denigrating. Mr. X. stated, "There is a part of me that just wanted to brag. . . . I really want this guy to say 'you're the greatest.' I thought how when I was an adolescent my father once said my cousin was amazing and I was so jealous. He never said that about me."

Mr. X. began the next session asking me if I could change the time of a session the following week. He went on to say that he was thinking about how much easier it was to accept yesterday's interpretation than it had been to accept other interpretations concerning his wishes toward his father.

Mr. X. paused. I understood him to be referring to the painful work we had done earlier in the analysis on his wish to be my homosexual lover, as well as his wish to be a woman and have me give him a baby. These wishes had been interpreted in both their negative and positive oedipal contexts. In regard to the latter, his wish to be a woman was associated with an adolescent masturbatory fantasy that his mother was bisexual and that he became her lesbian lover.

Mr. X. next reported that his father was having business difficulties. His request for a change of appointment was required because a number of family members were gathering to consider what might be done to improve his father's situation. He reported details of his father's failings as an executive, and jokingly said, "I am having a fantasy of taking over Dad's failing business and making it a success." I commented, "You sound as if you think you are ready to do that." He said, "yea" joyfully, and paused. His mood became more serious and he associated to the story of a boy who killed himself after his father called him an upstart for being critical of him. I interpreted, "You would like to be more potent than your father and replace him." Mr. X. said, "Yea. I understand that. Trying to think about it makes me very anxious. What I really want is to punish him for my disappointments as a child, to kill him."

From the organizing theoretical perspective that conceives of Mr. X.'s masochism as comprised of a complex of fantasies that are each best understood as a compromise formation, the analytic data from the two sessions presented in this chapter can be understood to reflect Mr. X.'s conflicts concerning his sexual and aggressive wishes toward his parents.

Mr. X began his session by reporting his masochistic fear of being humiliated. He did this against a background of hard-won analytic insight concerning both his wish to be humiliated and his wish to be a homosexual and a woman. These fantasies had been understood and repeatedly interpreted as compromise formations, resulting in a reduction of the agitated depressive unpleasure that characterized his personality.

In the sessions here reported the interpretations focused on the defensive aspect of one of these compromise formations; his fear–wish to be humiliated in the police station. The choice to emphasize the defensive function of the compromise formation in the sessions reported in this chapter was probably related to work on Mr. X.'s (sadonarcissistic) competitive desires toward his father. Their emergence and intensification at this time were related, in part, to exigencies in his father's life. It is important to emphasize that the theoretical perspective employed here stresses that this masochistic fantasy had other significance than being merely defensive. Sexual and aggressive wishes, as well as related wishes for punishment, contribute to the structure of masochistic fantasies. These other aspects of Mr. X.'s masochistic fantasies had been interpreted in earlier sessions. An example of such work occurred in the second year of the analysis. Mr. X. reported that during my summer vacation he had been plagued by the fantasy that he had AIDS. Analysis revealed both the wish for the experience of sexual love with the analyst as well as the wish to hurt and punish the analyst and himself. The latter self-punitive wish was understood to reflect, in part, his guilt related to the wishes gratified in his painful fantasy of infection with the human immunodeficiency virus.

In a sense it is a tactical decision that determines which aspect of a compromise formation an analyst chooses to interpret in a given session or series of sessions. The work in the two sessions presented here facilitated a diminution of the symptomatic unpleasure associated with his fear of being humiliated, and facilitated his more conscious experience of his positive oedipal competitive strivings. More specifically, Mr. X. became more aware of a series of sexual and hostile wishes (his [sadoexhibitionistic] fantasy of bragging, his [sadonarcissistic] desire for vengeance, and his wish to compete with and to kill his father). Mr. X. became more aware of how anxious these wishes made him. His associations to the story of the boy who killed himself after criticizing his father emphasize the self-punitive tendencies that are an important element of his conflict concerning his wishes to humiliate, hurt, and kill his father. Insight concerning these wishes diminished the unpleasure associated with them, as well as the related need to create a humiliating masochistic fantasy in the service of diminishing that unpleasure.

Although positive oedipal libidinal drive derivatives were not present in Mr. X.'s associations, previous analysis had demonstrated their contribution to the complex of compromise formations considered in these hours.

NARCISSISM

For decades confusion existed in regard to the meaning of the term *narcissism*. I have suggested (1980) that this confusion stems from Freud's (1914) two definitions of the term. Freud employed narcissism as a component of libido theory. In addition he defined narcissism as a fantasy of "perfection" (p. 94). I proposed that the definition of the term *narcissism* be limited to the latter sense. This facilitates analytic work with these ubiquitous narcissistic fantasies.

The quality of perfection may be consciously perceived or may be an unconsciously active, affectively powerful fantasy. The phrase "fantasy of perfection" is employed as a generalization. Fantasies of perfection are expressed in ideas of omniscience or omnipotence. A subject or object is thought of as most knowing, most powerful, most beautiful, most successful. What is common to all is a superlative designation, such as "most," and the absolute quality of this designation. Fantasies of perfection are also associated with the number "one," and often with the wish to be the "one and only." Fantasies of perfection are a ubiquitous aspect of human experience that leads to distortion of one's sense of reality, particularly as this relates to one's sense of vulnerability and finiteness. These fantasies differ from person to person in their elaboration and integration by the ego.

A limited definition of the term *narcissism* as a fantasy of perfection allows for a conception of narcissism as a compromise formation. Like all compromise formations it is composed of drive derivatives, unpleasurable affects, defense and superego elements interacting. Because analysis of a fantasy of perfection typically reveals a series of related fantasies, in every case one finds many different drive derivatives, many fears and miseries, many defenses and many superego manifestations in the underlying conflict(s).

The conceptualization of fantasies of perfection as a compromise formation leads to a number of clinically valuable generalizations. First, fantasies of perfection have a development that is influenced, in part, by the development of the calamities of childhood. Second, fantasies of perfection may function as defenses to diminish the unpleasure that is characteristic of the calamities and conflict. From this perspective a fantasy of perfection is one component of other, more complex compromise formations. Third, the threat of the loss of the fantasy of perfection evokes anxiety, while the sense the loss has occurred is associated with the experience of depressive affect.

Fantasies of perfection are to be thought of as developing in synchrony with the child's ideas of the imagined calamities of childhood, and are employed by its ego to diminish the unpleasure that characterize these calamities. For example, when a subject experiences unpleasure associated with the sense that love will be or is lost, fantasies of undoing the calamity may be associated with a sense that the subject is perfect and therefore lovable.

Analogously, when castration is threatened, or is imagined to have actually occurred, subjects may attempt to undo the sense of calamity by imagining they have a penis (Rado, 1933) or by imagining they can seduce (Loewenstein, 1957) or defeat the castrator. Similar fantasies characterize aspects of the child's masochistic and narcissistic (Rothstein, 1984) responses to the calamity of imminent punishment.

As with the calamities of childhood, once the oedipal epoch occurs, all the calamities and associated fantasies of perfection are usually so interwoven as to be virtually inseparable.

Fantasies of perfection are important aspects of the compromise formations that constitute the superego. The origins of the subject's ideals probably begin in the second year of life. However, once the child enters the oedipal phase of life, living up to his ideals and winning his parents' approval are inevitably linked to conflicts concerning the sexual and murderous wishes that characterize that epoch. For a child the sense of being able to win parental approval and love through performance or the sense of having manipulated, controlled, seduced, or defeated the punisher, often fantasized as sadistic and omnipotent, is associated with the conscious and/or unconscious fantasy that the subject is omnipotent.

At this point clinical material is presented and discussed to demonstrate the advantages that follow from conceiving of fantasies of perfection as being constructed of complexes of compromise formations.

Mr. X.* was the second of three children born in less than three years to parents who were often overtly seductive, humiliating, and disinterested in their children. He

*Analytic data from earlier phases of Mr. X.'s analysis was presented on pp. 63–65 to demonstrate the analysis of the subject's masochistic fantasies.

has been obsessed with bitterness and rage at his parents as well as with wishes for revenge.

Data are presented from a five-month period in the sixth year of his analysis which demonstrate some relationships between fantasies of perfection and the calamities of his childhood. In particular the data demonstrate the subject's effort to reduce his experience of depressive affect by pursuing fantasies of perfection.

Mr. X. began a session, two weeks before my summer vacation, by stating:

> For some reason I'm on this crusade to be perfect and I can't let it go. If the dinner I'm cooking doesn't turn out well I have a minor temper tantrum. When I ask myself what I enjoy, well, I enjoy skiing; but what I really enjoy is being admired from the chair lift. I think it's that I want everything. My law firm is so competitive. I respond with perfectionism and it robs me of any pleasure in it. I'm so angry I can't let it go.

The analyst interpreted: "You're angry you're not declared the winner by birthright." Mr. X. responded, "Yea, something like that. I think of my father not inviting me into his business." The analyst commented: "You believe that if you were perfect you could make your father want you as his successor."

Mr. X. responded,

> Yea, I still have that fantasy. I think, well, if I had gone to business school he would have done that. I feel like I'd have paid any price and would now be in my own firm. I suppose I do the same thing in analysis. I spent a fortune in time and money with Dr. M. (a previous analyst) and now I'm doing the same thing here in pursuit of the same fantasy. Most people would say, "Well you went through one really long analysis, try something else." All I do is

> come around to the same damn fantasy. I find yet another way to delude myself that if I only do the right thing I'll get my father's attention. It seems like the alternative is to be as depressed as hell. To give up this omnipotent fantasy. To give up the fantasy that if only I played my cards right I'd get his love. It feels like death. I cannot let myself feel what it feels like. It's as if thinking of the pain doesn't let one try. Thinking of being number one and wanting it and not getting it is too painful, so I say I don't really want it.

Three months later Mr. X. was struggling mightily to diminish the sadness he was feeling in response to his awareness that he was making progress in his analysis. He began a session by pondering the paradox of the sadness he felt in response to his professional success. The analyst interpreted: "You experience your success as a reminder of all the things you can't be and can't have." Mr. X. associated: "I say a resounding 'No!' to the idea of loss and disappointment. It's like some electric shock I can't consider inflicting on myself and then I think you think it bothers me and I say nothing bothers me because I'm the greatest." Mr. X. paused and continued: "One of the things about accepting that I can't change the past and about growing up would be I'll stop coming here and won't be with you anymore." Mr. X. associated to other losses and then said, "the idea that there are choices and that means leaving things behind and missing them every day I find unacceptable. It's like I won't be sad every day. I refuse! Then I get blocked." After a few moments of silence he said, "I immediately put the whole thing in terms of some kind of humiliation." The analyst interpreted: "You create a humiliator who you imagine you can beat. You imagine if you defeat the humiliator you won't have to deal with disappointment or loss." Mr. X. responded:

> I can really feel that and sense wanting to turn that into revenge and finally getting even. . . . The alternative is to

> say there's just loss, just disappointment. It's partly because I feel there is no comfort for that. Then I think there is comfort in going forward. . . . It's a measure of how much I still want from my parents that makes the idea of progress seem so bitter.

In the ensuing weeks the analyst was able to interpret Mr. X.'s narcissistic fantasies that if he did the correct thing he would be able to undo the frustrations of his life in general, and those of his oedipal experience in particular. The analysis of his experience of frustration in the transference was a particularly helpful vehicle in this interpretive process.

Mr. X. began a session six weeks after the one reported by saying:

> The idea that I had this operational fantasy that if I just worked hard enough I'd win my mother and have her all to myself seems crazy but right—so right! Today I feel myself in a real funk. It's as if I figured all the angles and still couldn't get my mother's love. Rather than just conclude that and say there are other things in life I feel there must be something I'm doing wrong and if I can only figure it out, I get my mother and be okay.

Mr. X.'s associations shifted to the fact that the Christmas and New Year's holidays prevented him from having five analytic sessions during those weeks. He stated:

> There being two three-day weekends in a row. I take it so personally. It's a three-day weekend for the entire United States and I take it as a personal failure and humiliation to not be able to get an appointment on Monday, and a humiliation that I can't get a senior partner to treat me as a special son, and a humiliation that I can't get my mother's love. I have to brood over it rather than just say that's the

> way the cards fell. Why do I feel I'll die when I don't feel I have the power, the control?

Mr. X. was silent for a while and said,

> Being a lawyer is satisfying in and of itself, but right now I feel so bitter. I can't win her love and that's just a recognition that I'm not omnipotent. So I'd like to say just go on and pursue your own interests but all day I feel angry, choking humiliation. So it was just a fantasy and that's what it was.

Mr. X. paused and the analyst interpreted: "You're experiencing a double disappointment. You sense the loss of the possibility of having your mother all to yourself, and the loss of your belief that you had the power to make it happen." Mr. X. responded, "the humiliation feels like shitting in my pants. I know my mother was enraged to clean my shit. Nothing I could do as a kid could make them love me. I stand back and look at it. It feels so bad so I revert to saying you can't hurt me."

The data from Mr. X.'s analysis emphasizes that conscious phenomena are associatively linked to complexes of related unconscious fantasies. These data stress that masochistic fantasies are always associated with conscious and/or unconscious sadistic and narcissistic fantasies that are also best thought of as compromise formations. The masochistic pleasure in pain, and/or humiliation or subjugation, is always associated with the sadistic pleasure in hurting, humiliating, subjugating and/or extracting revenge as well as with narcissistic fantasies of being the one who decides everything and of being the omnipotent humiliator, subjugator, and/or revenger.

The data exploring Mr. X.'s narcissistic fantasies of perfection stress the defensive function of these fantasies, as well as the relationship between the development of these fantasies and the calamities of childhood. Because of the latter relationship, analysis of fantasies of perfection inevitably reveals associative links to conflicts concerning childhood sexual and aggressive wishes. It is not uncommon in the analysis of fantasies of perfection to uncover associated bisexual fantasies. These too are analyzed as compromise formations and also function, in part, defensively. In men these fantasies may be expressed as the wish to be a woman, while in women they may be expressed as the wish to be a man. In both men and women fantasies of perfection and bisexual fantasies are not infrequently associated with fantasies of repair of a fantasied sense of defect and/or castration.

Finally, from the conceptual perspective that conceives of all fantasies in adults as compromise formations, the influence of parents, siblings, and other important people in the genesis of an adult subject's bisexual, masochistic, narcissistic, and sadistic fantasies is understood as one contribution in shaping their content. The real persons of a subject's world, and experiences with them, influence the content of the fantasies that constitute the subject's drive derivatives, affects, defenses, and self-punitive tendencies.

TRANSFERENCE

In the data presented from the analysis of Mr. X. reference is made to the subject's experiences of conflicts in relationship to his fantasies about the analyst. Mr. X. follows his report of his painful obsession concerning his uncle with an allusion to its meaning in the transference. He tells the analyst, "I know that it has to do with you." ("I know that my fantasies about my uncle are related to my fantasies about you.") Similarly, Mr. X. experienced very unpleasant fantasies of infection with AIDS in response to the analyst leaving him for a vacation. Mr. X.'s obsession was, in part, a displaced expression of conflicts concerning sexual and hostile wishes toward his analyst. These conflicts resonate with and are associatively linked to similar conflicts experienced in relation to his parents when Mr. X. was a child.

The term *transference* has a unique technical meaning in psychoanalysis. It refers to the fact that in the course of an analysis the patient experiences conscious and unconscious fantasies concerning the analyst. What is emphasized in these chapters is that all those fantasies are best understood as compromise formations involving, influenced by, and derived from childhood instinctual conflicts.

However, as Brenner (1982) has stressed, the subjects' fantasies in all their relationships are best understood as compromise formations. Every object relationship is shaped in this manner by the conflicts of childhood that are still active in later life. The relationship between patient and analyst in an analytic situation is no exception. Brenner has emphasized that there is nothing unique, nothing special about the fact that a transference relationship develops in every analytic situation. Every object relationship between, let us say, patient and doctor or other therapist has the same roots and is a similar compromise formation. What's unique about the relationship between patient and analyst is not its origin nor the fact that it develops as it does. What is unique is the way the therapist deals with or reacts to it. In analysis transference is analyzed. It is treated no differently from any other important compromise formation. The relationship of patients to their therapist is analyzed, rather than reacted to in any other way. Every transference in therapy, like every object relationship in any other situation in life, is ambivalent, is erotic, is aggressive, has its origins in childhood instinctual conflicts, expresses childhood sexual wishes, fears, miseries, has defensive and superego aspects. *Analysis* of the transference is not only vitally important, it is unique to analysis.

Chapter 5

Applications of the Theory of Conflict and Compromise Formation to Clinical Phenomena: Sublimation, Enactment, and Identification

Dale Boesky, M.D.

The notion of compromise formation is a theoretic construct which is intended to give a lawful explanation of human behavior. Thus we should distinguish the clinical phenomena which we can observe from the term *compromise formation* as a theoretic concept employed to organize

This material was first presented at the 1989–1990 "Seminar for Clinicians" of the American Psychoanalytic Association (see Dowling, 1991).

our understanding of these observable data. One will only be able to "see" a compromise formation by thinking in these terms and then deciding for oneself on the basis of experience if this was a useful way to think about the patient. The clinical examples of sublimations, enactments, and of identifications are presented to demonstrate further examples of the usefulness of compromise formation as a method to better understand patients.

SUBLIMATION

A man in analysis for conflicts which impaired his ability to work learned to play the clarinet as an adolescent. He took his clarinet with him one summer when he worked away from home and on lonely walks he stopped and played his instrument where no one could hear him. He recalled that one of the boys he lived with that summer distressed him by masturbating at night in such a way that he could be heard. Revolted by this the patient took his clarinet and again went off by himself to play. Later in life he collected recordings by clarinet virtuosos and took great interest in his son's clarinet lessons. When he was a child he was awed by the appearance in his home town of a famous jazz clarinetist and he treasured this musician's autograph. He loved many kinds of music rather indiscriminately and was especially fond of sentimental songs which often made him cry.

This man was terribly frightened by violent fantasies about competition with male rivals. His clarinet playing proved to offer him a disguised opportunity to express an unconscious masturbation fantasy in which he won the admiration of adoring crowds without risking direct competition with male rivals. In his sexual fantasies he imagined himself to be a woman so as to avoid danger from his rivals. This was expressed also in a fantasy of stealing his rival's strength by sucking on and then biting off the man's penis, swallowing it and using it for himself. His mouthing of the clarinet represented this wish in a disguised way. It was an acceptable way to allow him to gratify libidinal and sadistic wishes; it defended him against the danger of retaliation by other men; it allowed him considerable gratification in the sphere of reality as well as the fulfillment of important forbidden competitive sexual wishes related to his father and his son; yet when he played his instrument he felt that he was only a poor imitator of the real man who could really play well, and so he was punished by his failure. This attitude paralleled his chronic self-belittling attitude about his work performance compared to other men.

On one occasion the patient had a dream about the clarinet. He was at a dance. The clarinets were all in the front row of the band. One of the musicians was a little black boy who removed the clarinet from his mouth and imitated the sound of the clarinet with his voice. Then a former male teacher appeared in the company of two intimidating women and the teacher waltzed off leaving him alone with one of the scary women.

Thus the dream exactly paralleled his childhood and adolescent experience in which his father repeatedly left him alone to deal with the overwhelming conflicts induced by his mother's seductive and controlling behavior with him. As a consequence he could never feel pleasure in his penis if he touched it. He could only masturbate by rubbing his penis against the bed sheets and then he felt pleasure not in the shaft of his penis but in his perineal area.

So in the dream he could only be the little black boy pretending to be a real musician but never allowed to use the forbidden instrument. Both his sublimation and his dream represented more than the disguised expression of anguish: They were compromise formations incorporating his musical interest. But there are substantial differences in the comparative structure of these two compromise formations, as well as in their duration. The sublimation endured throughout his life, and the dream occupied but a moment of his sleeping thoughts.

ENACTMENTS AS COMPROMISE FORMATION

A woman in analysis was embarrassed to describe her wish to have her husband "do a certain sexual thing to her." All efforts by me to help her were to no avail. Gradually she became increasingly angry and demanded that I should say something more. She was tired of doing all of the talking and hearing nothing more from me to show whether what she said had any meaning or importance. When I asked her if she might be embarrassed about telling me about this sexual matter, she felt that I was patronizing her and tried to embroil me in an argument. When I asked if she might be annoyed with me because telling me about this sexual matter seemed to be distressing her, she denied this, and insisted that my interest in why she wished me to speak expressed my needs rather than hers. All that she wanted was that I should just talk to her. Obviously she did not mean that literally since I was indeed speaking to her. At about this time she blurted out that what her husband did was to perform cunnilingus on her. It was then possible to help her to see that her actions with me that have just been described represented more than just a defense; they expressed the defensively disguised forbidden wish to get me also to use my tongue on her, by forcing me to talk. This wish was forbidden because it had specific incestuous and sadistic meaning for her in the transference. Notice also that it is merely the frame of reference which governs whether or not to describe her enactment as expressing a forbidden wish, or as a transference resistance, in that she wanted me to talk instead of telling me her exact thoughts and wishes. In this instance both are relevant and accurate. Her acting in the transference in this manner allowed her to achieve several purposes simultaneously. In the service of the prevailing wishes, she gratified forbidden sexual and sadistic fantasies. In the service of defense, she avoided painful feelings of guilt by projecting the blame of causing pain on to me, and by covering her guilty fear of punishment with concerns about embarrassment. Furthermore, her superego interests were gratified because she invited punishment by trying to provoke me into becoming angry with her, or inviting me to be unkind to her. Considerations of reality were highly important as well, in that it was her actual task as a patient in analysis to communicate to me as best she could just what it was that was distressing her. It is typical that when we view resistance as a compromise formation, we can then see that the patient who thinks he is being uncooperative is consciously unaware that the apparent misbehavior is actually highly communicative and valuable.

IDENTIFICATION

A man in analysis for a severe depression revealed in various ways during a lengthy analysis that he unconsciously wished to be like his mother for a variety of reasons. One of the most important problems had to do with his father's severe emotional problems, which required lengthy psychiatric hospitalization when the patient was thirteen. The subsequent failures of the patient's older brother in his adult life rekindled the traumatic conflicts about defeating his male rivals which were originally evoked by his father's collapse and subsequent failures. His mother had a highly ambivalent attitude toward his father and her sons, and expressed this by encouraging all of them to rely on her for everything possible. She was the one who cleaned up everyone's mess, and his father was a bitter man who blamed everyone else for his unhappiness. Gradually the patient's mother took over the family business altogether. Illegally, she kept two sets of books, one false set for the official tax inspectors, and the other for her actual needs. She did not have to raise her voice to get her way. She was very skillful at manipulating people, in contrast to his antagonistic, abrasive father.

In the analysis the patient also, figuratively speaking, kept two sets of books, just as his mother had. He consciously withheld reporting details of his sex life and delayed reporting other important matters for lengthy periods of time. When I would ask him about his often telling me only months or years later about important experiences and events, he mockingly dismissed the significance of his behavior. He treated his business partner in the same manner as he treated me, in that he was quietly hostile and controlling but outwardly cordial. Thus he controlled his business partner and his analyst exactly as his mother had controlled her family. All the employees knew that if they needed an answer they should come to him, rather than to his partner. He also had a deeper motive for assuming the position of strength with which he had, in his fantasy, endowed her. He was unconsciously convinced that he was merely an extension of his mother, and that he could not exist independently without her. For this reason, when she died he was unable to shed a tear, and his identification with her was strengthened so that he could in fantasy keep her alive within himself. His entire sense of adequacy depended on the approval of his mother, or later, other persons who symbolized her to him. His identification with his mother, intertwined with his profound dependence upon her, gradually became one of the most important resistances in the analysis. By imagining that he was just like her, he fulfilled a group of complex wishes. He achieved sexual and hostile gratification by defeating me when I represented his father and older brother. If he could have the analysis on his terms, just as his mother had controlled his father, he could defeat me. For many years he had been resentful about all the doctors he knew whom he felt were so superior to him. By withholding information from me, he defensively avoided frightening and depressing issues linked to his dangerous fantasies. By floating forever in the timeless illusion that all his needs would be gratified by me with no effort on his part, he also fulfilled the wish to have his mother restored to him in the treatment. At the same time that his feminine identification spared him the wrath of the male rivals, he was always vulnerable to depressive affect because he felt like a fake man, and this was his punishment for having outdone his father and his brother. We can thus discern the diverse achievements of his compromise formation in which he lived out the fantasy that he was his mother.

Chapter 6

Principles of Psychoanalytic Psychotherapy

Homer C. Curtis, M.D.

Some psychoanalysts are of the opinion that psychoanalysis cannot be clearly distinguished from psychoanalytic psychotherapy, except by such quantitative factors as number of sessions, regularly scheduled for a set amount of time, and, perhaps, a longer duration. However, when compared according to the quality of the process certain significant differences can be recognized. Granted that these differences are likely to be blurred at the border where an intensive psychotherapy may acquire some descriptive and qualitative characteristics of psychoanalysis, there remain distinctions of importance in the patient's experience and the nature of the interaction between patient and analyst, as well as the technical interventions that both bring about and result from this shared experience. Some of these differences can be related to the respective goals of the two therapeutic categories, especially if we step away from the borderland back to the definitive ground typically granted to each. The names themselves point to one dimension: therapy versus analysis. While obviously never mutually exclusive, except perhaps at the extreme ends of the spectrum, the aim of therapy emphasizes alleviation, relief, adjustment, and return of function. While such developments will occur in analysis they are not by themselves considered as endpoints, but are subjected to further exploration to determine their meaning and function. This means that the emphasis has been shifted toward the aim of increased self-knowledge and capacity to continuously expand the awareness of the inner psychic life. For this process to be initiated, established, and maintained requires a special constellation of technical measures that make up the psychoanalytic situation. These include the use of free association ranging over the entire psychological field, rather than goal-directed discussion; the recumbent position; regularly scheduled appointments four or five times a week; the analyst's attitude of empathic objectivity, tolerance, and neutrality toward the patient's productions; abstinence from participating in the patient's extra-analytic life or in his transference enactments; and dealing with the latter primarily by clarification and interpretation. While there may be variations among these elements at different times, they form a relatively constant configuration conducive to the emergence of previously unrecognized or poorly comprehended thoughts, feelings, and fantasies, now more available for insight, modification, and integration into the mature personality.

Any alteration or neglect of any of these elements of the psychoanalytic situation can have significant effects on the nature of the material the patient produces and on the quality of the interaction with the analyst. This is particularly true of the effect on the two central dynamic forces, transference and resistance, the analysis of which can be impeded by deviation from the optimal balance of these basic technical features. It is, in fact, selective change in this ensemble of attitudes and procedures that can either make for *poor* analysis or *good* psychotherapy. Thus it can be most useful to have a working understanding of the human psyche, the consequences of the approach to the patient, and the technical interventions, in order to match the patient's realistic and psychological needs with the selection of a psychotherapy most likely to be effective in reaching his goals.

A major contribution of psychoanalysis not only to psychotherapy but also to the field of psychiatry, indeed the whole field of medicine, is the psychodynamic way of thinking. This takes into account the influence of unconscious mental forces, interacting dynamically with processes of defense, affect, and ideation to reach an accommodation that is more or less adaptive. An understanding of the nature and meaning of these processes makes possible not only the choice of treatment to fit the patient's needs and capacities, but also an appreciation of the unique and highly variable solutions and compromises each person reaches. This expansion of one's grasp of this inner world of impulse, feeling, and fantasy promotes at once a tolerance and fascination that allows us to listen, learn, and perhaps resonate with this other human being in ways that are in themselves therapeutic.

In making the distinction between psychoanalysis and psychotherapy it should be stressed that this is for the purpose of providing a scientific and practical frame of reference within which an informed choice of an optimal psychotherapy can be made. In fact, from a strictly practical and therapeutic point of view the need for developing increasingly scientific and utilitarian applications of psychotherapy is of paramount importance. The role of psychoanalysis in this endeavor is analogous to laboratory research in discovering principles that can be the basis for development and application on a broad scale. Psychotherapy, properly applied, should not therefore be considered second class, or only a choice dictated by realistic limits. Often enough it is evident that a carefully selected form of psychotherapy may be the treatment of choice for certain forms of psychopathology. I will provide some suitable examples of this.

To set the stage for this let me remind you of some of the points made in previous chapters regarding conflict and compromise formation. These concepts are useful representations of universal mental processes that are efforts to achieve some equilibrium that satisfies the wishes and demands of all aspects of the psyche. Symptoms, character traits, dreams, and transference are all compromises of varying degrees of complexity, expressing elements of wish, unpleasant affects, defense, and punishment. In any form of therapy, indeed in any human encounter, there exists the potential for altering the form of a compromise formation by some shift in the relative strength of these various components. Either in a spontaneous, unwitting social relationship, or in a scientific, planful psychotherapy, a person with a painful or crippling compromise formation may use aspects of the encounter to feel more gratified, less anxious and/or less depressed, safer, relieved of guilt. On the other hand, they can feel disapproved of, punished, deprived, and so on. In any case, it is possible that previous symptoms, traits, and inhibitions may change in degree, disappear, or be replaced. Freud referred to such phenomena when he said that more patients were cured by religious conversion than would ever be cured by psychoanalysis. If the therapist is seen as a good parent who offers support, comfort, safety, forgiveness, and permission, the balance between the components of the compromise is apt to change, often with symptom relief. Or, the therapist is able to mobilize and help the patient utilize an existing psychic resource or tendency with the result that a new and more adaptive equilibrium is reached. In more intensive, expressive forms of psychotherapy with relatively high frequency and long duration, the personal interaction between patient and therapist provides a unique opportunity for a new experience in human relatedness. More effective modes of behavior may be learned through trial and error in the safer, permissive atmosphere of the treatment, and when integrated by identification with the therapist can result in lasting personality changes.

All of the foregoing shifts and modifications also occur in psychoanalysis. The additional dimension provided by analysis lies in the expansion of awareness into underlying areas of conflict thereby subjecting childhood impulses and defenses to the repeated scrutiny and modifications worked through by more mature, objective, and effective mental processes.

The selection of patients for a specific psychotherapeutic approach depends on an evaluation of their need for and capacity to initiate the various processes of change just described. Some of the characteristics favorable for psychoanalysis include an awareness of suffering or dissatisfaction combined with a wish to understand oneself through self-observation. This is usually associated with a tolerance for frustration and good impulse control. A history of capacities to work productively and to maintain relationships with others is reassuring, as is evidence of a sense of humor and capacity for metaphor. As a rule, acute crises in the current life situation are not conducive to the wide-ranging, consistent self-reflective method of analysis.

Using this set of characteristics as a model, we can derive a picture of the patient for whom psychotherapy would be a better choice. Upheaval and crisis are indications for supportive, problem-solving measures, at least until a state of relative control and calm allows an assessment of individual resources and limitations. Difficulties in impulse control and frustration tolerance, often evident from a history of problems in work and relationships, are reasons for recommending a supportive, educational therapy. Limits in ability to reflect on one's thoughts, feelings, and behavior are often revealed by the patient's refusal to follow up an invitation to observe himself. This limitation would favor a supportive and directive type of therapy, rather than one aiming at insight and conflict resolution.

Obviously, reality factors of time, place, and expense may be decisive. In addition, different combinations of the qualifications described for the two major categories of psychotherapy may dictate an intermediate form of therapy combining expressive and supportive features.

In order to illustrate these principles and to demonstrate how psychotherapy can selectively use certain aspects of psychoanalytic theory and technique in order to fit the treatment of the patient's specific needs, I will first present the highlights of a psychoanalytic case, followed by several psychotherapy cases in which various principles and techniques were combined to treat specific clinical problems.

The first patient was an intelligent twenty-five-year-old woman in the entertainment field. In spite of increasing success and recognition she had begun to feel depressed, irritable, and tense. In addition, she had recently come to question her very active sexual life, marked by frequent conquests of the men she encountered in her acting career. These problems seemed related in time to a somewhat stormy relationship with a man she had seduced and with whom she then became seriously involved. Her sexual conquests had been experienced as casual and satisfying, more from the sense of power than from the strictly sexual aspect. While her affairs had been a means to advance in her career, she did not see herself as being used but felt herself to be using the men for her purposes.

Her considerable common sense told her that the man with whom she was involved was a person of superior qualities in every way and was a worthy choice for marriage, which she had set as an ultimate goal. Yet she never felt completely at ease with him, and against her better judgment found herself teasing and mistrusting him. Realizing she was in danger of losing him and, importantly, sensing some perverse need to push him away, she sought help through analysis.

In her accustomed way she approached the analysis with vigor as if to conquer her illness or to wrest victory from the analysis. This attitude served her well for several months as she explored her history and behavior at length. While she gained a better sense of control and a broader perspective on herself, she realized that real understanding and change in her puzzling behavior still eluded her. There followed a period of increasing interest in me and my private life, and it both pleased her and made her envious to attribute to me all kinds of special knowledge and accomplishments. These feelings soon became erotically tinged, and her behavior became first covertly, then overtly, seductive.

When this behavior developed into such a diversion and preoccupation that she frequently lost sight of her analytic goals, I pointed out to her the similarity between her actions in treatment and her characteristic way of trying to seduce and conquer every man of any importance to her. I further suggested that it was understandable that she would feel impelled to rely on a familiar way of mastering anxiety when confronting a new and threatening situation in the analysis. This clarification of her counterphobic character defense, repeated and expanded over several weeks, led to a remarkable shift in demeanor. Heralded by disturbing dreams of being chased or attacked, she began to dread coming to the analytic sessions and began to feel anxious and self-conscious on entering the office. She dressed more conservatively, and her body language became more modest. After becoming aware of frequent bouts of blushing, she observed that she was feeling like a frightened virgin.

This marked change from bold seductress to frightened virgin I understood to be the emergence of a transference neurosis, that is, a regressive and dystonic expression of aspects of warded-off childhood fantasies, now focused on me in a revived, yet modified, form of conflictual object relationships of childhood. This affective experience is by no means identical with that of childhood, since the latter has undergone elaborations and transformations and now occurs embedded in an adult personality engaged in a real therapeutic relationship. It is nevertheless remarkable that both major themes and specific relationships from childhood can be so closely approximated and affectively relived.

The extent and nature of the transference neurosis may vary widely from patient to patient. In some, it is a florid, gripping experience difficult to contain within the analysis, leading to acting out or flight. In others it appears as a pallid, attenuated, "now you see it, now you don't" kind of experience that is contained within safe limits by character defenses that work only too well. Such manifestations might better be called transference phenomena rather than transference neurosis, which implies a more organized, abiding, psychic structure. At times the recognition of the transference neurosis may be delayed or blurred since a predominantly defensive aspect such as stubbornness or apathy sometimes appears rather than the more obvious drive and affect qualities. With other sources of information such as dreams, fantasies, memories or, often more importantly, the analyst's empathic responses or countertransference, these states of resistance can be seen as being as much a part of a transference neurosis as the more obvious erotic or angry states. Conceptually, they represent what Anna Freud called transference of defense since they are derived from defenses that originated in the child's effort to establish equilibrium and control over threatening impulses.

In the patient I am describing, the anxious, breathless, blushing state was explored with the help not only of the patient's dreams and associations but also of my empathic responses. Images of a frightened doe and a sense of impatience in my reaction were clues suggesting that she was struggling with a masochistic fantasy in which I was to be the sadistic attacker. Several different versions of this interpretation resulted in increasingly clear manifestations of the fantasy in dreams and conscious images.

With the appearance of memories and dream elements referring to a specific house in which she lived at age five, it was possible to begin interpreting the genetic connections and to reconstruct a more cohesive picture of the development of her neurosis. For example, she recognized the experience of anxiety in the analytic session as identical to her phobic feelings in childhood, which began shortly after repeated exposure to scenes of parental intercourse. Initially, this was expressed as a fear of her father. She would run away from him when he came home, in an anxious, excited way, only to have him chase her. This was a good example of a compromise formation in the form of a symptomatic act, in which her anxious running provoked her father to chase her. It is of interest that the patient's efforts to find a more comfortable solution to her conflict over her masochistic misconceptions of the feminine sexual role took not only a neurotic form but also a more sublimated one. In her phobic isolation as a child she frequently resorted to romantic fantasies and acted the part of the heroine in familiar fairy tales and stories. In her adolescence she overrode her shyness and anxiety to take part in school plays, which then led to her entertainment career. Her activities in the theater became increasingly satisfying and absorbing. She first lost the original feelings of anxiety and later the driven counterphobic quality, a transition that made acting more tolerable for her. At the same time that these changes were occurring, however, she developed the counterphobic sexual promiscuity that eventually led to her seeking analysis.

This telegraphic and condensed segment of a five-year analysis can serve as a paradigm for a number of additional transference themes that were developed and explored: rivalry with an older brother; hatred for the father who didn't love her enough; identification with the victimized mother who, in reaction, could sadistically control men by seduction—all were worked through and related to her drive to seduce men. The relationship with the man which precipitated her anxious depression could not be sustained for long; and it was not until late in the analysis, after she had worked through the transference sufficiently, that she began a relationship that eventually led to marriage. This period was especially fruitful analytically since it demanded careful scrutiny of her transference feelings in contrast to her increasing capacity to comprehend and follow through on her mature sexual aims, which were now being freed.

Important features of this brief and condensed case report are the choice of a patient with discernible intrapsychic conflict embedded in a personality structure with good adaptive capacities. Providing a stable, safe therapeutic situation allowed the use of free association to get in touch with previously warded-off psychic contents and processes. This is usually associated with anxiety about regression and loss of control, leading to reliance on, and clinging to, familiar symptoms and character defenses as a kind of first line of defense. These are dealt with by clarification, which helps the patient grasp some of the patterns and meanings of these familiar kinds of behavior. As these become less automatic and more uncomfortable, transference manifestations are likely to become more evident. These are expressions of previously repressed feelings and fantasies of childhood. The experiencing, observing, and understanding of this mixture of revived and reactive modes of expressing conflicted longings now occupy the center stage of analysis and are dealt with by interpretation and reconstruction of their origin.

In contrast, I will now describe an example of a psychotherapy case using some aspects of an analytic approach, but with significant differences.

A forty-year-old physician came for help in dealing with feelings of depression, exhaustion, and anxiety that he was not able to provide good enough medical care to his patients. Out of his fear that he might miss a diagnosis or make a mistake that would hurt a patient, he felt compelled to be available to his patients at all times. He could not allow himself to take vacations or even a weekend to be with his family. He felt guilty about this neglect of his wife and children, which added to his feelings of depression. Because of his mental turmoil and the physical exhaustion resulting from his overworking himself, his neurotic worry about hurting his patients was now in danger of realistic fulfillment. It seemed clear that he was conflicted over sadistic impulses to inflict pain (the origins of which lay in some early childhood experiences) and was trying to counteract this by driving himself to avoid any possibility of hurting his patients. I understood his oversolicitude about his patients' welfare to be a guilty willingness to sacrifice his own health and welfare. Accordingly, I pointed out to him that in his loyalty and dedication in providing the best medical care for his patients he was actually in danger of impairing his ability to be of greatest help to them, since he was becoming increasingly exhausted. I suggested to him that he could be of greater help to his patients if he would rearrange his work schedule to allow for more rest, with occasional vacations and attendance at medical meetings to keep him current with the latest advances in medical treatment. This would mean arranging for other physicians to take care of his patients while he was away, a difficult decision for him to make since it meant giving up temporarily his obsessive watchfulness to avoid harming them. However, as I was able to help him realize that his wish to avoid harming his patients would be better served by a schedule that would make him more alert and in a better physical, mental, and professional state to help rather than harm his patients, he was able to carry out this plan. As might be expected, his obsessional tendencies were expressed in his way of arranging and carrying out his new schedule, but in this form were much less crippling.

This psychotherapy lasted about four months, and the patient's relief from depression and anxiety has lasted for a number of years. The crucial therapeutic action was a shift in the conditions he set for himself to try to control his guilt over sadistic impulses. Instead of avoiding guilt by trying frantically to attend to every symptom of all his patients all the time, which led to depression and exhaustion, he came to realize that this might actually end up hurting his patients. By leading a more balanced life of looking out for his own health and keeping up with advances in medical knowledge he could reassure himself that he would help and not harm his patients. In other words he would now feel guilt over possibly hurting them if he were to continue his previous maladaptive mode of avoiding feelings of guilt.

Obviously, the intellectual awareness of the logic of making such a change in his neurotic style of caring for his patients was in itself not sufficient. It took several months of empathic listening and clarifying the painful cycle he was caught up in for him to develop a sense of trust and confidence in me as a kind of good parent. This attitude of positive transference not only gave me some leverage to help him change his mode of controlling guilty feelings, but also was the basis upon which he could make an identification with his perception of me as a good doctor–parent who wanted to help patients (including himself) in a calm and consistent way, with benign skill rather than frantic oversolicitude. This identification with me was the stabilizing cement that held together his newfound clinical approach to his patients.

If we compare this psychotherapy case with the previous psychoanalytic vignette, we can see important differences. Beyond the obvious differences in frequency and duration, the second patient was a more rigid, constricted personality, with less capacity to reflect on his inner life and subject such self-observations to inquiry and analysis. I considered him less able to tolerate regression and further loosening of his character defenses, and relied more on efforts to reestablish his obsessional modes of control. This was accomplished by clarification of his behavior patterns and facilitating his displacing his ineffectual mode of controlling his guilt by oversolicitude and overwork, to the more effective mode of increased mental and physical energy, plus pride and confidence in his medical skills. Interpretation of repressed material was avoided, and transference feelings were limited to his experiencing me as strong, benign, and an idealized physician. This fostered an identification with me that seemed to integrate his self-image in a stable, more consistent way.

Another vignette will illustrate a different clinical problem requiring a different psychotherapeutic approach. This patient was a forty-year-old unmarried and socially isolated woman chemist who found it increasingly difficult to do her work, partly due to trouble getting along with her immediate superior, but also due to her reluctance to keep up with current developments in chemistry. She developed anxiety spells, insomnia, and depression in association with her work inhibition. I saw her twice a week for approximately a year, focusing first on her experience on the job, then expanding our exploration to her personal relationships past and present. In addition to the relieving effect of being able to ventilate her feelings to another person for the first time in her life, she also examined at length her experiences with the important people in her past history. She proved adept at delineating the quality of her characteristic ways of interacting with people, and soon found a common theme of resentful competition, especially with men. She realized that her educational and professional strivings were based partly on a need to prove that she was as good as a man, not inferior as she seemed to fear. Because this way of combatting feelings of inadequacy meant competing aggressively with men, conceived of as hurting them, she felt anxious and guilty. To avoid these painful feelings she inhibited her competitive impulses, thus interfering with her ability to do her work. She soon realized that this pattern of feeling and behavior stretched back into her early reaction to a younger brother who was born when she was four. From the time of his birth he was favored over the patient, who accepted this as proof that to be loved one had to be a boy. So she set out to be as masculine as possible, developing her mind as if it were a phallus. As she realized that this was one driving force of her professional ambitions, it became clear to her why she had to inhibit them. She became increasingly able to separate this childhood motive for working from the more mature motives of intellectual satisfaction and earning a living, and gained considerable relief from her work inhibition.

In comparing this patient's therapy with the psychoanalytic case, we see more limitations in this woman's flexibility and capacity to deal with personal relationships, especially with men. This had led her to limit her social contacts and opportunities for sharing feelings and problems in mutually supportive ways. This was provided by the therapy in a carefully monitored way to avoid the development of too great a dependence. At the same time I emphasized the value of efforts to expand her social circles by pushing herself to join church groups and professional societies. As her depression lifted and her confidence increased she was able to take these steps to establish a social life for herself. No attempts were made to interpret the unconscious dimensions of her social inhibition, which shared the same roots as her work inhibition. The main technical procedure in this therapy was what is commonly known as clarification. This consists of a careful scrutiny and delineation of persistent personality traits and behavior, along with the associated ideas and feelings. These are often only vaguely known to the patient, being simply considered "givens," automatic reactions in familiar social situations. They are not unconscious processes that have been repressed, but they often escape conscious notice. However, with repeated self-scrutiny and the therapist's observations, they can be experienced more acutely, tied up with other character traits, and led back historically to provide a more cohesive picture of one's personality and development. While this does not lead to emergence of repressed conflict it does clarify derivatives in the form of character defenses. This can lead to a sense of one's cohesiveness and a feeling of self-knowledge and mastery, conceptualized in a stable verbal form.

There are some patients who for reality and psychopathological reasons do not fit the indications for either psychoanalysis or supportive psychotherapy. This may require a creative combination of techniques that provides support and a new interpersonal experience within which self-esteem and insight can be increased. While not allowing access to unconscious dynamic and genetic factors, working for a considerable period of time with the derivatives of those underlying elements promotes personal growth and self-understanding. One such patient was a twenty-eight-year-old male graduate student hampered by social anxiety, study inhibition, and bouts of depression. His progress toward a doctoral degree had been delayed by these symptoms, and he had on several occasions been on the brink of dismissal from his graduate program. He had several male friends who shared his intellectual and musical interests, as well as his rather isolated social life. His sexual life had been limited to relationships with four or five women with whom he managed barely satisfactory sexual relations, but without real intimacy. He despaired of finding a woman who would want to marry him, since he realized his anxiety and mistrust could be alienating.

As might be expected, he had much difficulty committing himself to therapy. His anxiety had an edge of alertness and mistrust that we both understood to be the immediate obstacle to therapy as well as a major, long-standing problem. His occasional wry humor about his mistrust reassured me that it did not reach paranoid proportions. Understanding that both frankness and sensitive restraint were essential, I told him that I thought he would benefit most from an intensive, long-term therapy that would give him the opportunity to understand and overcome his fear of being trapped or humiliated. I suggested further that we could start on a trial basis, with the understanding that if he found he did not trust me he should feel free to discontinue. This escape-hatch gave him some sense of safety, while my recommendation for intensive therapy reassured him that I recognized his need for help.

We began on a twice weekly schedule, sitting face-to-face, exploring both his daily experiences and his reactions to me and the therapy. The first few months were clearly a testing period in which he looked for, and occasionally found, justifications for questioning my intentions or ability to help him. More than I might ordinarily be with a patient, I tried to be alert to my inner feelings and my reactions, realizing his sensitivity. My mistakes and misunderstandings were confronted and discussed frankly, not only for clarification but also to understand his experience of my imperfections. Within limits, I would answer his questions about such things as my vacations, my office decorations, or my automobile. If I felt his questions were too personal, or if answering them might interfere with the therapy, I would tell him so. He would smile and agree.

The cumulative effect over the first six months of this approach was one of gradual relaxation of his guardedness. He felt more confident that I would not pounce on him, use his words against him, or try to dominate him. He now could begin revealing to me some of his secrets, fantasies, and painful memories of childhood. His increased trust in me, based on his experience with me while explicitly examining and understanding that experience while it was happening, was now further enhanced by linking his mistrust to remembered traumas and abuse. Since our psychotherapeutic approach did not produce the kind of material that would elucidate his projections and transformations of his traumatic experiences, we were content with the reconstruction of a coherent picture of his development up to the present. His symptomatic improvement, increased self-confidence, and sense of direction enabled him to complete his dissertation and graduate. His relations with women became freer and more intimate and he seemed headed for marriage when I last heard from him.

This therapy lasted three years and consisted of two major elements. The first was what Bibring (1954) called "experiential manipulation" in which the patient is provided with opportunities, both within the treatment and without, to have new experiences that can have mutative effects. These are made possible by the permissive, encouraging atmosphere of the therapy and the leverage of the transference. In this case the transference was not analyzed as it might be in psychoanalysis, although the transference experience was discussed and utilized to clarify the patient's way of relating to therapist and other people.

The second element of technical importance was the clarification of his patterns of behavior, and their derivation from past developmental influences. This reconstruction differs from that provided by psychoanalysis in not having the dimension of unconscious conflict and fantasy explicitly integrated into it. However, it can provide a sense of cohesion and self-understanding that has a stabilizing effect.

From the discussion of psychoanalytic principles and concepts of mental functioning, plus the clinical examples presented, we can derive some basic technical suggestions for psychoanalytic psychotherapy:

1. Identify the crucial dynamic issues in order to localize and limit the therapeutic effort.
2. Do not interfere with aspects of personality that are not closely related to the central problem.

3. Focus on the patient's current relationships and character defenses.
4. Support the patient's adaptive skills and resources.
5. Provide a stable, receptive atmosphere of support and respect.
6. Encourage more adaptive solutions to previously ineffectual, painful symptoms through new displacements and identifications.

At the point in therapy where the patient has shown some stable improvement, a decision to terminate must be considered. The limited goals of psychotherapy require that regression to dependence on the therapist be controlled by supporting and encouraging the patient's pride in his efforts at independence. Evidence of growth and increased ability to function should be recognized as an accomplishment deserving of respect. The patient's wish to terminate usually is accompanied by some anxiety that can be alleviated by the therapist's agreement and confidence in the patient's capacity to maintain the improvement.

These comments and recommendations are meant to serve as general guidelines and must be supplemented by further study. However, the most important learning must come from the actual experience of working over time with patients. This allows the development of an individual style of therapy that comes out of repeated trial-and-error experiences.

Chapter 7

Child Analysis: Its Origins and Clinical Characteristics

Scott Dowling, M.D.

A hallmark of psychoanalysis is the psychological importance accorded to childhood in general and to childhood sexuality in particular. This is most notable and evident in the neuroses of adults, but has equal applicability to normal character development and expression. One result of this emphasis on childhood is a view of human psychology which stresses the continuity of infancy, childhood, adolescence, and adult life. Psychoanalytic data indicates that psychological life progresses in successive, interdependent levels of complexity through a process termed epigenesis; each level grows out of the past and contains transformed elements of that past. In psychoanalysis we find the child in the adult and pay particular attention to the transformations that characterize the stepwise movement from infancy to adulthood. In the psychoanalysis of a child we engage ourselves with the child in hopes of favorably affecting his future as a productive and innovative person and as a satisfying and satisfied sexual partner and parent.

The two fundamental pillars of psychoanalytic theory are the existence of a complex, motivated, unconscious mental life and the determinative importance of childhood. A corollary finding is that the needs, wishes, fantasies, gratifications, disappointments, humiliations, and danger situations of childhood, and their transformations, are retained in the unconscious and have lifelong importance.

The two drives, sexual and aggressive, which underlie the major motivational systems, interact with each other and with the pressures of conscience, self-esteem regulation, and social and physical requirements in ways which are frequently conflictual and which lead to the manifold and varied expressions of needs, wishes, and fears, in both adults and children.

In the previous chapters, you have read about the fundamentals of psychoanalytic technique, especially the importance of free association, resistance, transference, and countertransference.

You may well ask, "How are these analytic theories and concerns applied to work with children?" How can a manifestly adult activity, as therapeutic psychoanalysis assuredly is, with its emphasis on immobility, introspection, insight, and a special capacity for delayed gratification, be applied to children who, either in whole or in part, lack all of the attributes or capacities just listed? I will return to this question after providing some historical background.

Sigmund Freud was no stranger to children. Among his other early neurological accomplishments was a textbook on cerebral diplegia, which we call cerebral palsy in the United States. This book was the product of many years of working in a children's neurological outpatient clinic in Vienna, one of the positions he filled during the lean years after leaving Brücke's laboratory. There he worked with and observed many children and their parents. At home, he fathered and cared for six children of his own and, as his correspondence makes clear, he frequently asked about and collected anecdotes concerning the children of his friends and colleagues. In 1905, not long after publishing his initial findings concerning childhood sexuality in "Three Essays on the Theory of Sexuality," Freud undertook the psychological treatment of Hans, the five-year-old son of one of his young colleagues (Freud, 1909). This was no ordinary treatment and certainly was not an analysis. The boy's father took notes on what the child said about his phobia of horses and about other matters and passed them on to Freud who, in turn, advised the father about directions to take in his discussions with his son. Freud met and talked with the child on one occasion. In Freud's report, it is immediately evident that the family life was not happy; the parents competed for the affection of the child. The mother was sexually seductive and stimulated Hans's jealousy and competition with a baby sister. Hans, like most children his age, was quite able to tell about the content of his thoughts and feelings. What is notable is that his father and Freud listened and treated the child's words as serious communications from a young mind. Even today, few of us are willing to treat children with such respect.

What the boy described, and Freud records in his paper, are a series of fantasies, beliefs, confusions, jokes, and heartfelt concerns. Many of these centered on the mouths of horses, who he felt were going to bite him if he came close, and on the possibility of horses falling down. Other ideas centered on feces and on the pleasures and concerns associated with producing or retaining feces. Hans found many analogies between the making of feces and his faltering and largely fantastic ideas about the origin and birth of babies. Finally, both the thoughts concerning the biting mouths of horses and the many ideas about feces were organized around his deep affection for and sexual interest in, as well as his competition with, each of his parents. He wanted to "coax" with his mother and straightforwardly competed with his father to be able to do so; he also wished for the exclusive love of his father. He had many ideas about male and female genitals which emerged in his play about horses and in pictures he drew of a giraffe. In his simple and straightforward thoughts, Hans supported many of Freud's ideas about childhood sexuality, as presented in "Three Essays on the Theory of Sexuality."

Freud's interest at that time was not in developing child analysis, which he really doubted would be possible. He was seeking confirmation, through observation, of his speculations and reconstructions from work with adults. He made similar observations of his own six children and later, his grandchildren, and collected the observations of other parents concerning the fantasies and beliefs of their children. He believed these observations could confirm or modify his reconstructions from the analyses of adults, and could provide details and evidence of psychologically important issues that might be missed in working with adults.

It was Anna Freud who first moved toward the analysis of children (A. Freud, 1928). Anna, the youngest of Freud's children, was trained as a teacher, but had been conversant with psychoanalytic ideas through listening to her father's conversations with visitors. She first attempted to solve the problem of gaining the interest and participation of young children by making promises to relieve their symptoms, or by demonstrations of power and knowledge. But the technique she used was not impressive as a form of psychoanalysis; she made unabashed use of suggestion, direction, and educational devices. Anna Freud's therapeutic ideas were challenged by a young Hungarian analyst, Melanie Klein, who sought to reproduce the conditions of adult analysis by substituting play actions for the free associations of adults (Klein, 1923). She felt that drive interests, resistance, and superego attitudes could be interpreted solely on the basis of the child's play activities which she believed were governed by unconscious, repressed interests. She also introduced novel theoretical ideas which I will discuss in the next chapter. The struggle between the ideas of these two young women became a major international debate within psychoanalysis. The pendulum eventually swung strongly in Anna Freud's direction, not only because her father was Sigmund Freud but for two other reasons as well. With Berta Bornstein she developed a technique that eliminated both the use of promises to induce the child to accept analysis and purely educational techniques as an important therapeutic technique. Instead, she analyzed defenses against the awareness of affect, that is, she brought the child's attention to ways in which his or her feelings were being distorted or suppressed. For example, anxiety, fear, envy, and anger could be recognized behind overly friendly or subservient or withdrawn behavior. The *means* through which the child avoided conscious recognition of the emotion was gently pointed out, often with the subsequent appearance of the emotion in question. Or, both the means (defense) and altered affect might be interpreted. In this way, the treatment opened up previously hidden topics of emotional significance for further discussion and analysis. From this beginning she went on to extend Freud's notion of defense, demonstrating the clinical importance of many describable forms of defense.

Some years later (A. Freud, 1936) she published a book, *The Ego and the Mechanisms of Defense*, summarizing her work over the previous decade. Her studies of therapeutic work with ego functions and their interaction with drive and superego functions effectively outlined the direction of psychoanalytic research and development for many years to come. The impact of her clinical material and lucid presentation were highly persuasive. In this book, the *means* through which the personality seeks to restrain, deflect, forget, alter, or displace feelings, impulses, and fantasies is again the focus of attention. These means were described as attributes of the ego; they were the "mechanisms of defense" and were an important aspect of the "resistance," a topic that we have previously discussed. Defense analysis was necessary to both adult and child analysis; it was an effective means of engaging children in the process of analytic therapy.

Though originally viewed, somewhat dismissively, as a "women's activity," child analysis bloomed in the heady, liberal, postwar atmosphere of Vienna in the 1920s and 1930s. It was a time of liberation from old monarchial traditions, often led by Jewish intellectuals. Frequently inspired by the social ideals of communism and socialism, young men and women turned to the new psychoanalytic psychology of individual worth as a blueprint for radical change. During the 1920s and 1930s, psychoanalytic ideas were applied with great impact in the fields of delinquency, education, and child rearing. The new psychology inspired a group of young analysts who joined with Anna Freud in developing specialized analytic techniques with children.

Much of the forward momentum of child analysis, as of psychoanalysis as a whole, was dissipated in the horrors of World War II. The Jews of Vienna were decimated in the bloodbath of anti-Semitism; Freud's books were publicly burned and psychoanalysis banned. Freud and his family were hounded by the Gestapo. One of his sisters died of starvation in Theresienstadt, while the other three are believed to have been murdered in Auschwitz (Gay, 1988). Freud, his wife, his sister-in-law, and Anna barely managed to escape to England in 1938. Freud died the next year, in 1939.

In wartime England, Anna Freud established a group living setting for preschool children who were separated from their parents; then, the war over, she established the Hampstead Clinic which became the international center of psychoanalytic training and research with children.

Unlike adult psychoanalysis, child analysis was inspired not only by one-to-one psychoanalytic treatment and research but also by a humanitarian tradition of interest in the welfare of children. Child analysis has always had an active involvement in the life of children in settings other than the consulting room. Child analysts in the United States work in the nursery school, elementary schoolroom, pediatric hospital, and residential treatment center as well as in one-to-one analytic relationships. As a result, child analysts are observers of children and advisors to their caretakers and teachers as well as therapists. They combine the results of informed observation and the findings from analytic therapy of children and adults in their theoretical and clinical formulations.

Psychoanalysis, whether of adults or children, shares a common goal, the integrity and psychological success of the individual. This goal includes respect for oneself, a capacity for love, both sexual and affectionate, and an ability to work and learn.

Childhood sexual love progresses through a series of phases or organizations; the principal objects of that love are the parents. An understanding of the nature of childhood love is essential to a knowledge of psychoanalysis. I will take a few minutes to outline its major phases and characteristics.

The first organization of the *libido*, the psychoanalytic term for sexual energy or interest, is the oral or mouth-centered organization of the first year or eighteen months. Intaking activities of the mouth, and, later, aggressive biting and expulsive spitting are typical oral activities. But orality also includes tactile, visual, and olfactory intaking, grasping, and rejecting activities.

Anal activities, with special emphasis on the opposing pleasures of expulsion and retention and of messiness and orderliness, are important features of the anal organization during the second and third years. Just as other intaking and other pleasurable activities were a part of the oral organization, so issues of control, motor skill, and autonomy are important ingredients of the anal phase.

Phallic organization, prominent in the third to fifth years, is marked by intense pleasure in exhibitionism, intrusive curiosity, and genital masturbation on the one hand, and deeply felt anxiety for bodily integrity and danger (castration anxiety), on the other. Closely associated with the phallic organization is the Oedipus complex, a deeply experienced, excruciatingly confusing, genitally oriented, love and hostility felt toward both parents. Each parent is loved deeply, yet each is also seen as the prime competitor for the love of the other parent. The child's resolution of this universal dilemma, when successful, includes a greater degree of autonomy and self-direction, the formation of an inner representative of parental authority which we know as the conscience, and a relative decrease in the intensity, awareness, and openness of sexual attitudes toward the parents. The sexual nature of the child's interest in his parents is "transformed" into a more distant, affectionate interest and the intensity of curiosity and intrusiveness and competitiveness is "transformed" into a growing interest in peer relationships, school, and organized physical activities. Invariably in untroubled children, but more extensively in children with disturbed development, aspects of the oedipal dilemma are repressed; the oedipal conflicts become an organizing ingredient of unconscious thought and, as such, they contribute to unconscious fantasies which may become the determinative wellspring of neurotic disturbance.

The years from about six to ten or eleven are known as "latency," a time when the intensity of sexual pressure is relatively quiescent. With preadolescence, from ten or eleven until age thirteen, we again see confusion and intensity of sexual feelings, which then become more organized, peer directed, and specifically genital during the adolescent years.

This digression about childhood sexuality, in which I emphasized the early phases, is intended to clarify what is meant by a child's capacity to love. A child's inability to reach and traverse each of these phases, and to do so with a loving parental partner or partners, constitutes, in psychoanalytic parlance, a developmental disturbance. But what of the capacity to work, which we also mentioned as a goal of psychoanalytic treatment? In the case of a child, this means a freedom to learn, to play, and to participate, cooperatively, with others. A sequence can be outlined for the developmental line from the self-directed play of infants, through the various types of childhood play, to the assumption of responsibility and the pleasure in creativity in the work life of an adult. We view the individual's pleasure in work as an important ingredient of psychological health.

From what I have said, it is evident that, without exception, it is the individual with whom we are concerned in psychoanalysis. Although the social system in which the child and adult lives is recognized as an important and necessary influence with which he interacts, the goals of the state are explicitly subsidiary to the goals, needs, and satisfactions of the individuals who make up the state. Prejudice or the sacrifice of individuals for the state are incompatible with psychoanalysis.

I will now describe, in more detail, the techniques and problems of child psychoanalysis at different age levels. In the psychoanalysis of school-age children and adolescents, the use of a couch is optional and, when the child wishes to lie down on it while speaking to us, we attempt to understand with him why he wishes to do so. Often the reason has more to do with "trying out what it feels like to be a grown-up here" or with assuming a passive role with the analyst, than an attempt to use the couch in an analytically helpful manner. Older children usually sit in a chair in my consulting room; younger ones often sit at a table with me in a children's alcove where paper, pencils, and a few simple toys and games are available to him or her. These arrangements are similar in individual psychotherapy with children; psychoanalysis differs in its outward form from psychotherapy in that the child sees the analyst more frequently, four or five times a week. During analysis, the actions of the analyst are quite specific and deliberate, though one hopes not stiff or unnatural. Every word, every action, every gesture is devoted to the single purpose of facilitating the child's awareness of motives, of thoughts, of feelings, and of actions which serve purposes foreign to his intended, conscious wishes. This atmosphere is created by being interested and attentive, not by promises or declarations. The child and his utterances are treated with seriousness and respect, often for the first time in his life. Within this framework of commitment to the child, and to working with him, there is constant attention to those details which will help the child know himself better. As mentioned in connection with Anna Freud, this often takes the form of comments about defensive distortion of affect, particularly in the early days or weeks of treatment. Let me give you a few brief, ordinary examples.

> An eight-year-old came to my office for the third time, talking as rapidly as possible and leaving me no opportunity to interact with him. When I finally had a chance to speak, I commented that it might be his feelings about being in my office that got him speaking so rapidly; that sometimes kids get concerned about what it's going to be like talking with me.

> A ten-year-old boy who was having serious difficulty in school, and in forming relationships with other children, rarely mentioned these problems in his meetings with me, though he often was forced to talk about them with his teacher. In a similar but reverse manner, intense anger at his parents was expressed to me but never to his parents. And, as he eventually told me, he often complained to his parents about me. Segments of his life were kept very separate from each other, shielding him from a consistent awareness of feelings of inadequacy and helplessness, thus preventing him from taking any steps that would change his situation. In speaking to him, I asked if he had noticed the way in which he kept parts of his life separate as if in separate rooms. His experiences in school are kept in one room; his feelings and experiences with his friends in another; those with his parents and with me in still others. He rarely remembers, thinks about, or gets help with the "room" he's in at the moment. I wondered why this was so; it really made it hard for him to get help with anything. I suggested that it would be valuable for him to know why this happened because then he would be able to do more to help himself.

The analytic attitude of attentive concern includes acceptance of verbal and motoric expression, but not unlimited satisfaction of impulse, either aggressive or sexual.

In child as in adult analysis, we follow the principle of "abstinence"; by this we mean that there is a relative absence of direct sexual or aggressive gratification of either patient or analyst in the analytic setting. Children often move about the office; they may demonstrate a physical skill such as how to hold a tennis racket or do a dance step; they may play a game or draw a picture or discuss their schoolwork. In each instance the analyst accepts these age-appropriate activities, but also may use them as occasions for recognizing what is expressed in the activity—be it competitive ambition, a wish to please the analyst, a desire to demonstrate mastery, a countermeasure to feelings of anxiety or guilt, an occasion to obtain disapproval or punishment or, more likely, some combination of the above. Issues of tact, timing, and relevance in relation to overall issues in the analysis also enter into decisions that are made by the analyst about what to say and when to say it.

> A twelve-year-old boy who felt an intense lack of caring love from his parents had many symptoms of an oral nature. In the work with me he often expressed excruciating hunger which could make him restless and unable to concentrate on anything else. He sometimes relieved his longing by going to the bathroom in my office and getting a drink of water.

Gratification by drinking water was allowed. On the other hand, I did not feed him and helped him to understand that his wish that I provide him with food was also a wish for gratifying, protective care from me. I also helped him see how that wish was an extension of similar wishes with his parents, both in the present and in the past.

> A seven-year-old girl who had been subjected to destructively overcontrolling and sexually stimulating behavior by

her parents was regularly demanding and controlling in her daily hour with me. She insisted that I sit in a particular place, that I say a particular thing, that I play a particular game, that I "be happy." After noting the controlling aspect of this behavior many times, I suggested that she may have other feelings as well. She became anxious and spoke about thoughts that I might do something to her that she wouldn't like. When I continued to refuse to become an active participant in these games, she described situations when she controlled her dangerous and sometimes hurtful father by instigating games with him.

Despite the repeated experience that unconscious fantasies can be brought to consciousness, and their influence on the child's life reduced, analytic work with children raises many questions. Most analysts believe children lack certain psychological characteristics that are integral to adult analysis. For example, transference involves the reliving of past experiences in present-day relationships. The school-age child is still a part of the parent–child relationship; those relationships have not yet become a part of his past. Furthermore, because of an immaturity of cognitive capacity, the school-age child has a limited capacity for self-observation and insight. Child analysts, such as myself, believe that, despite these limitations, the child is capable of using the analytic relationship and the recreations of past and present conflicts within the analytic relationship in a manner which is helpful to him or her and is also useful in making generalizations about the psychological life of children.

Although the seven-year-old girl, mentioned earlier, saw me predominantly as a helpful, even maternal person, she could bring many elements of the frightening relationship with her father into the analysis, as indicated by her fearful efforts at controlling me. Though she never fully objectified the nature of the relationship with her father, she could recognize her excitement with him and a similar excitement with me and did, eventually, help herself by distancing herself from him rather than by trying to control him directly.

Adolescents show marked differences from younger children in the lability of their emotional state and in their growing capacity for objectivity and insight. Difficulties in working analytically with children of this age group are related to the intensity of their sexual and aggressive urges and to conflicts associated with their wishes to be cared for by others. I rarely use the couch with adolescent patients, because of their conflicts about passive homosexual wishes. In adolescence, a need for separateness from adults can precipitate sudden departures from treatment. In spite of the problems inherent in working with adolescents, this can be a most rewarding group of patients. Finally, psychoanalysis is used with preschool children as young as two to three years. Although "analysis" with these children is both therapeutically helpful and has provided important insights into the psychology of childhood, its form is so different from analysis with older children or adults that it is best understood as a special form of treatment in its own right. Play, directed by the child, is used extensively, and interpretations make use of play themes. In talking with these young children, their sometimes diffuse, "preconceptual" thought, as originally described by Piaget (1951) and illustrated by Bornstein (1935) and Fraiberg (1959) in the psychoanalytic literature, provides a startling window into the fantasy world of the young child. With this age group, as with Freud's patient, Hans, there is ready access to fantasy which will later exist primarily in unconscious forms, though it will continue to be evident in dreams. Fantasies of oral impregnation, of anal or umbilical birth, of fecal gifts, of sadistic oral and anal wishes, and of oedipal desires and distress are often directly expressed.

As the final topic in this chapter, I would like to briefly discuss countertransference in child analysis. Countertransference reactions are the unconsciously determined responses of the analyst to his patient, usually on the basis of earlier responses to emotionally important figures in the analyst's past. Countertransference is a particular problem in work with children. There is a tendency to idealize the child, to take his side in relation to the parents or, conversely, to take the parents' side in relation to the child. There is a tendency to disregard or minimize the intensity of the child's emotional life. The child can come to represent unrealized aspects of the analyst who may try to relive unhappy aspects of his own childhood through his patient. Or the child may represent despised aspects of the analyst who may then reject or punish his patient. The child's passivity, or his controlling activity, may stimulate the analyst's desire to restrain and control him in a sadomasochistic fashion. The motoric freedom of child analysis makes it easy to rationalize punitive or gratifying behavior. The answer to these countertransference problems lies in the effectiveness of the child analyst's own analysis and in his continued willingness to recognize and examine his motives and actions.

In this brief description of clinical child psychoanalysis I have stressed three issues: the importance of a detailed knowledge of child development, the complexity of clinical issues such as transference and countertransference in work with children, and the bedrock importance of the analyst's respect for the value and integrity of the minds of children.

Chapter 8

Child Analysis: Applications and Contributions

Scott Dowling, M.D.

In this chapter I will discuss applied analysis; it includes data from settings other than the "psychoanalytic situation" between patient and analyst in the consulting room. Psychoanalysts are wary of applied analysis because of possible distortions and distractions from the central issues of psychoanalysis, the origins and expression of unconscious conflict as discovered in the psychoanalytic situation. Although the criticism is valid in many instances—a great deal of nonsense is presented to the uninformed public as psychoanalysis—no description of psychoanalysis, particularly of child psychoanalysis, would be complete without recognition of the profound influence it has had on diverse aspects of our society.

For example, psychoanalytic studies of blind children have revolutionized the understanding and preventive treatment of the developmental deficiencies commonly associated with blindness (Fraiberg, 1977). In other areas, such as infant developmental research or the organization of day care facilities for infants and children, the contribution of psychoanalysis has been a part of a general cultural trend which has included influences from pediatrics (Kempe and Helfer, 1980), academic psychology, and the child welfare movement. All of the applications which I will discuss in this chapter could not have occurred without supportive data from the psychoanalytic treatment of children or from observational studies by psychoanalytically informed observers. The changes instigated by psychoanalytic research reflect a continuing psychoanalytic insistence on the importance of childhood to the social and intellectual, as well as to the moral, well-being of a society. Yet, the average adult, including the average psychiatrist treating adults, politely but firmly dismisses the significance and complexity of childhood. Perhaps it is because we have all survived childhood and wish to leave it behind us, while life as an adult seems so much more powerful and immediate. Psychoanalysts who have studied this phenomenon believe there are unconscious reasons for the dismissive attitude. We suggest that it is the same complexity and emotional pain of childhood that draws some psychoanalysts' interest that also makes it necessary for others to distort, smooth over, and minimize the importance of what has been and can be learned concerning the normal development as well as the conflicts and distress of that period of life. Most adults, particularly male adults, are as committed to the idea that childhood is simple, naive and forgettable as they are to the proposition that it is asexual.

Freud himself, to whom we are in debt for bringing us face to face with the fact of childhood sexuality, occasionally expressed similar dismissive attitudes. Freud and other early analysts saw work with children as an educational activity; they believed that only women were suited for the task; and suggested that children were sufficiently naive to accept lies about the intentions of the analyst.

They did not yet understand, as we know today, that the emotional and cognitive awareness of children, though different from that of adults, is nevertheless both acute and complex. In spite of these early aberrations, our present awareness of the deep and continuing mystery and significance of the psychology of infancy and childhood; our respect for children as unique individuals who require at least as much consideration and care as we provide to adults; and our overriding conviction that any serious student of adult psychology must study the child as well as the adult, are all products of our Freudian legacy.

The most extensive and direct contribution of child analysis has been in the detailing of psychological development. Though much of what I will describe includes an element of controversy and continuing uncertainty, these are simply the characteristics of an expanding and difficult science as compared with belief systems which can afford the luxury of absolute certainty. Unlike adult analysts whose research proceeds by the collection of psychoanalytic data within the psychoanalytic situation, the child analyst, when considering the infant and toddler, utilizes direct observation. Freudian analysts believe that there is incomplete structuralization of the infant's and toddler's mind into a drive-dominated impulsive id, an organized, executive ego, and a value-dominated, punishing or rewarding superego. These structures of the mind develop through processes of maturation and internalization of experience over many years; observational studies of preverbal children are required if we are to understand the mind prior to structure formation and if we are to understand the sequence of steps which leads to the structured adult personality.

Infants without Families (A. Freud, 1941) is an early example of this work; it is a study by Anna Freud and her colleagues of their experience in England during World

War II with young children separated from their parents. In it we learn about the specific ways in which development suffers when, in spite of conscientious attention, a child lacks a devoted, singular caretaker. Under these circumstances children may learn at a very young age how to take care of themselves but with associated inhibitions of exploratory behavior; they similarly use restricting forms of defensive avoidance to deal with distressing or challenging events. René Spitz (1945) extended the implications of this work in his studies of infants raised in well-organized, clean institutions, which offered adequate nutrition but did not provide the loving ministrations of a mothering person. He described a high incidence of morbidity and mortality among these infants, a finding that has had a profound influence on the organization of infant services in Europe and the United States. Spitz's emphasis on trauma was expanded by colleagues (Kempe and Helfer, 1980; Steele, 1982) to highlight the previously unrecognized high incidence of physically and sexually abused children.

Both these groups of studies stressed the importance of the relationship with the mother or other primary caretaker to the well-being of a child. The elaboration of the nature and the importance of that relationship has been the subject of continuing controversy and research. Actually, the controversy began twenty years prior to the publication of *Infants without Families*. Melanie Klein, whom I mentioned briefly in the previous chapter, believed that the mind of the young infant is the arena of an early and complex struggle between the forces of *eros* (love) and *thanatos* (death). These terms were used by Freud to indicate general instinctual forces, found throughout nature, and expressed in humans by loving and destructive impulses. Klein believed the primal forces of love and death found complex expression in the child's early relationship to the mother and were represented in the mind of the child by primitive fantasies of loving merger and annihilating destruction (Klein, 1975). Although she did not describe an interactive relationship between mother and child, her emphasis on the importance of the mother as the object of the infant's presumed erotic and destructive impulses has led others to consider her the originator of object relations theory.

It was Anna Freud and her followers who made many of the important observations concerning the actual relationship between mothers and infants; they have utilized these observations to formulate exceedingly helpful descriptions of child development from infancy to adult life. Anna Freud's concept of developmental lines (A. Freud, 1963b) was a means of combining knowledge of sexual and aggressive drive development with the new discoveries concerning the ego's defensive and adaptive characteristics. Each developmental line defines a sequence of developmental events that includes consideration of drive, ego, and superego factors. For example, the developmental line from suckling to rational eating considers the behavioral steps along the way, such as weaning, self-feeding, use of utensils, and reduction of nonrational attitudes to food, and defines the psychological requirements and results of each step. When discussing irrational attitudes to food, the early equation of food with mother and the influence of normal, infantile sexual fantasies such as oral impregnation and anal birth must be considered. When these beliefs are unconsciously retained beyond the third or fourth years, there may be interferences with feeding, such as a fear of poison, a fear of getting fat, and reaction formations against oral, sadistic, biting attitudes.

A diagnostic scheme of childhood psychological disorders and a protocol for developing and formulating a psychoanalytically informed diagnosis during childhood were other valuable clinical tools developed at the Hampstead Clinic (A. Freud, 1963a).

Another approach to development from birth to four years was advanced by Margaret Mahler, a Hungarian American analyst, and her colleagues (Mahler, Pine, and Bergman, 1975). This work focuses on the early forms of attachment to the mother and on the developmental line through which the child comes to terms with his separateness and individuality from the mother. Of particular importance was her description of a child's ambivalent awareness of separateness during the period from eighteen months to two years. Children at this age are not only pleased with their ability to do things on their own, they are also aware that in doing so they are changing the comfortable and safe closeness they have previously enjoyed with their mothers. Many analysts still believe that the borderline conditions of later childhood and adult life have their origin in disturbances of this period.

Another important contributor to our understanding of early relationships is Donald W. Winnicott (1958), a British analyst who has roots in both the Freudian and Kleinian traditions. He did not seek to establish a separate school or form of child analysis. His books and papers are characterized by evocative, poetic writing as he attempts to capture the emotional and cognitive intensity, diffuseness, and vulnerability of the infant and young child. Although his work lacks the conceptual rigor of many other analytic investigators, most would agree that he has come closest to capturing in words the experience of infant and parent during the early months of life.

Daniel Stern (1985) is representative of a modern group of investigators of infants and of infant–mother relationships. Utilizing the latest of technological instrumentation, they measure and record every detail of an infant's movements, his motoric and physiological responses to stimuli, his preferences and capacities. From these data, Stern and others have visualized an infant with significant independent capacities at or near birth, including the capacity for interactions as a separate, though very immature, self. In his view, the traditional Freudian division of the personality into id, ego, and superego has been replaced by an emphasis on an increasingly complex sense of self engaged in forming intersubjective relationships with others. Other child analysts, though recognizing the significance of Stern's observational data, do not concur with his theoretical conclusions (Solnit, 1987).

Alongside the studies which have directly investigated the mother–infant relationship have been other studies focusing on specific aspects of infant and toddler drive or ego functioning. Selma Fraiberg, an analytically trained social worker, discovered that many of the repetitive, socially inhibiting actions of congenitally blind children such as rocking and stereotyped movements, mutism and echolalic speech are direct effects of a failure of appropriate emotional stimulation and not indications of brain damage (Fraiberg, 1977). These behaviors have uniformly been successfully prevented by enlarging and enriching the experience of the blind child with its mother in specific ways.

Selma Fraiberg introduced me to the developmental psychology of Jean Piaget, the renowned Swiss investigator. Piaget was psychoanalyzed by Sabina Spielrein, the most original and tragic of all Russian psychoanalysts; she is reputed to have been a victim of Stalin's purge in the 1930s. For a time Piaget retained an interest in psychoanalysis, then turned from it as a guide to his own work. Nevertheless, his early books are replete with psychoanalytically inspired examples and studies, particularly in his discussion of children's dreams (Piaget, 1951). His later studies have been of value to psychoanalysts when considered in conjunction with psychoanalytic studies of affect and motivation.

The effects on normal development of congenital disturbances other than blindness have also been studied. Deafness, abnormalities that prevent oral feeding or anal elimination, disturbances of skin sensitivity and awareness of pain, and motoric limitations have been the object of investigation within a psychoanalytic framework (Dowling, 1977). There have been positive results for reducing psychological abnormalities in affected children and for our growing understanding of the developing mind.

The point of this review is that child analysts and associated professionals are pursuing the mysteries of infantile psychological life with increasing energy and sophistication, often combining psychoanalytic knowledge and techniques with information and techniques from other, related sciences. Though there continue to be more questions than answers, the deluge of revelations concerning early life and the practical applications of many of those findings to the care of infants has been a source of excitement and satisfaction.

Female sexual development, which Freud declared a weak point in his theory, has been clarified to a great degree by the combined observational and clinical analytic findings of the last ten to fifteen years. Exaggerated views of women as forever feeling defective and inferior to men, as focused on the notion of being castrated males, as having unstable and relatively weak superegos, and as partially frigid if their orgasms originate from clitoris as well as vagina, have all been modified or set aside on the basis of psychoanalytic data from both the psychoanalytic situation and from direct observation. In many instances, these changes have destroyed straw men, ideas that, in fact, Freud later changed himself. In other instances, the criticism has been valid; these are instances of correction and change which are a part of any scientific endeavor.

There have been related changes in our view of gender awareness. As with infant studies, much of this work has been done by nonanalysts. John Money, a nonanalytic psychologist, did the early work in this area (Money and Ehrhardt, 1972). Psychoanalysts such as Phyllis Tyson (1982) have supported and advanced Money's view which places the establishment of basic and permanent gender assignment in the first year to eighteen months, and have also worked out details of gender development during the subsequent months and years.

Young children sometimes require psychological treatment for severely interfering disorders. Inhibitions of functioning such as mutism or inability to make friends; developmental fixations as indicated by encopresis or enuresis; psychophysiological disorders such as juvenile asthma; and neurotic disturbances are examples. In Cleveland, child psychoanalysis or child psychotherapy is provided by private practitioners or by a private psychoanalytic clinic for school-age and adolescent children, where charges for treatment are based on the parents' ability to pay. For children from two to five years of age, there is a therapeutic nursery school providing specialized help for children with these conditions. Parents meet weekly with a therapist who helps them clarify their own feelings and fantasies concerning the child and assists them in finding ways to support the child's psychological growth. Observations of the child in the nursery school setting and the provision of psychologically supportive experiences in the school are essential ingredients of the therapy. Similar programs in a number of other American cities are modeled on the Cleveland experience. Two books of special interest which are based on data from these young children are *The Therapeutic Nursery School* by Robert Furman and Anny Katan (1969), which describes the results of treatment, and *Not by the Color of Their Skin* by Marjorie McDonald (1970), which reports on a psychoanalytic study of the psychological basis of racism as it occurred in the setting of the therapeutic nursery school.

I will now turn to the influence of child analysis in several nonclinical areas. The first of these is the care of children in the home. Dr. Benjamin Spock's books and talks on parental care of children have been enormously influential for more than thirty years. Recently, he has been displaced as America's most influential pediatrician by Dr. Berry Brazelton. Both Spock and Brazelton have received training in psychoanalytic settings; both combine psychoanalytic ideas with pediatric information and emotional support in their advice to parents. The emphasis in their advice is on the value of parental confidence, respect for the individuality of the child, and loving firmness in the upbringing of children. They recognize the forcefulness of the child's drives, the importance of shaping the derivatives of those drives toward individual fulfillment and social responsibility, and the importance of adult supervision and affection in directing the child's energies to those ends.

This attitude of respect for the child is also evident in changed forms of pediatric care, especially in hospitals. James Robertson (1952, 1958, 1968, 1969, 1971), and James and Joyce Robertson (1967, 1971) created a series of annotated movies that forcefully document the psychological pain endured by children who have been removed from their parents for hospitalization or for other reasons. As a result of their studies, provision for the psychological needs of hospitalized children has been vastly improved. In most U.S. hospitals, parents are welcome as partners in caring for their children, and specially trained child care workers support and prepare children for medical procedures, provide education when appropriate, and encourage play activities which enable children to master experiences which would otherwise be lastingly painful. Emma

Plank (1962), a leader of this movement and an early student of both Maria Montessori and Anna Freud, founded a multidisciplinary organization, American Association for Children in the Hospital, to further this development. It is a happy memory that I, as a young psychiatrist, was part of the group who assisted Mrs. Plank at that time. This is now an international organization with thousands of members, known as The Association for the Care of Children's Health.

Another important effort to further the place of children in our society was the publication of a book, *Beyond the Best Interests of the Child* by Joseph Goldstein, a lawyer, and two psychoanalysts, Anna Freud and Albert Solnit (1973). They coined the term *psychological parent* to refer to the person to whom the young child has made an attachment and on whom he has become dependent for his physical and psychological well-being. Thus, a psychological parent may be a mother, a father, a grandmother, a foster parent, or other involved, caring adult. They suggest, and the courts have often agreed, that when there is an issue of custody of a child, as in a divorce, or when a parent dies, or when adoption is being considered, the decision of the court should be based not on legal considerations of prior right or genetic relationship but on a determination of which adult has achieved or is likely to achieve the position of psychological parent for the child. The rule of law is designed to protect the rights and freedom of the individual and to support the family in providing care to children.

> The child's body needs to be tended, nourished and protected. His intellect needs to be stimulated and alerted to the happenings in his environment. He needs help in understanding and organizing his sensations and perceptions. He needs people to love, receive affection from, and to

> serve as safe targets for his infantile anger and aggression. He needs assistance from the adults in curbing and modifying his primitive drives (sex and aggression). He needs patterns for identification provided by the parents to build up a functioning moral conscience. As much as anything else, he needs to be accepted, valued and wanted as a member of the family unit consisting of adults as well as other children [pp. 13–14].

> Only a child who has at least one person whom he can love, and who also feels loved, valued, and wanted by that person, will develop a healthy self-esteem. He can then become confident of his own chances of achievement in life and convinced of his own human value. Where this positive environmental attitude toward an infant is missing from the start, the consequences become obvious in later childhood and adult life. They take the form of the individual's diminished care for the well-being of his own body, or for his physical appearance and clothing, or for his image presented to his fellow beings. What is damaged is his love and regard for himself, and consequently his capacity to love and care for others, including his own children [p. 20].

Child analyst Bruno Bettelheim survived Auschwitz to become a champion of the individuality and integrity of children. He founded the Orthogenic School in Chicago for children who would otherwise have been placed in state hospitals, and helped many of them (1950). He was also a wonderful writer; his book *The Uses of Enchantment* (1976) is about fairy tales and their value to children. He defends the value of fairy tales of danger and aggression, of wicked stepmothers and avenging giants. He sees in them an opportunity for the child to recognize his own impulses and fears as a part of something outside himself. In the resolution of the story, the child has an opportunity to see that such terrible issues can be mastered and overcome. His lessons are ones for all of us who face dark and difficult times. Our literature and cultural heritage provides an opportunity to recognize the possibilities of redemption and progress while also recognizing, with Raskolnikov (the tortured central character of Dostoyevsky's [1916] *Crime and Punishment*), that a murderous, desperate element universally inhabits the human heart.

> [P]arents fear that a child's mind may become so overfed by fairy-tale fantasies as to neglect learning to cope with reality. Actually, the opposite is true. Complex as we all are—conflicted, ambivalent, full of contradictions—the human personality is indivisible. Whatever an experience may be, it always affects all the aspects of the personality at the same time. And the total personality, in order to be able to deal with the tasks of living, needs to be backed up by a rich fantasy life combined with a firm consciousness and a clear grasp of reality [p. 118].

> A particular story may indeed make some children anxious, but once they become better acquainted with fairy stories, the fearsome aspects seem to disappear, while the reassuring features become ever more dominant. The original displeasure of anxiety then turns into the great pleasure of anxiety successfully faced and mastered [p. 122].

I will end these two chapters on child analysis where I began. Psychoanalysis should not be equated with a specific set of detailed propositions about psychological life, either normal or pathological. Basic to the psychoanalytic ideal is a scientific attitude of objectivity, submission of theory to evidence, and renunciation of authoritarianism. But equally basic to psychoanalysis is a specific assumption concerning individual life and freedom. The most basic requirement of psychoanalysis is a belief in the worth and integrity of the individual. This must be an absolute personal value of the psychoanalyst for psychoanalytic therapy or research to take place. Total confidentiality, assurance of privacy of communication, and freedom from all outside interferences must be assured or psychoanalysis is a sham. Who would share their most intimate masturbation fantasies, their murderous intentions and erotic desires, their intensity of ambition, and their depths of guilt and shame without absolute assurance that the mind and the mouth of the analyst are sealed? Without this assurance there can be no psychoanalytic data and without psychoanalytic data there can be no psychoanalytic theory. This is a burden for the analyst; a vulnerability and a loneliness that is inseparable from the honor of being admitted into the privacy of the minds of others.

Chapter 9

Psychoanalytic Perspectives on the Treatment of Sicker Patients

Sander M. Abend, M.D.

We will now discuss the application of psychoanalytic principles to the treatment of sicker patients. There is confusion about diagnostic criteria, and controversy about etiology in respect to this group of patients. Theoretical differences among the schools of psychoanalysis, and between psychoanalytically oriented psychiatrists and those who are uninformed or unsympathetic to psychoanalysis, complicate the study of these clinical problems still further. I want to be clear about one thing from the beginning; I do not feel that psychoanalysis in any form, or even psychoanalytically based psychotherapy, is the best way to treat schizophrenic patients, or those suffering from affective psychoses. Freud and the psychoanalysts who followed him have always been interested in what our methods and theories might be able to tell us about psychotic patients. Today, most efforts to apply psychoanalytic ideas to the treatment of sicker patients are limited to work with patients whose illnesses lie in the diagnostic borderland between the classical neurotics and the severely ill psychotics.

I will sketch some of the history of psychoanalytic thought about severe mental illness, including psychoses, because this will help to make clear where some of the etiological controversies and diagnostic confusion come from, and prepare us to see where and how the psychoanalytic approach can fit into the treatment options with some sicker patients. From the beginning there has been uncertainty about the roles played by constitutional factors, environmental biological influences, and psychological experiences of all kinds in the production of these syndromes. Aided by technological advances, research in neuroanatomy and neurophysiology is constantly changing our picture of mental functioning in health and disease. Even the great clinical psychiatrists who worked before the introduction of Freud's ideas were concerned about diagnostic issues. Kraepelin (1913) and Bleuler (1911) saw patients who were not hospitalized, and who suffered from milder forms of some of the symptoms associated with severe psychoses. Today, *The Diagnostic and Statistical Manual of Mental Disorders* (DSM-III) has a specific but limited category for what is called borderline personality disorder (American Psychiatric Association, 1986). It is based upon a purely descriptive definition that includes impulsive behavior, lack of control of anger and/or intense anger, impaired relations with others, volatile mood swings, disturbances in the sense of self and identity, and feelings of emptiness. A number of other diagnostic categories in DSM-III designate other varieties of severe personality disorders and some milder forms of psychosis, but those patients are not considered borderline in the strict diagnostic sense of DSM-III. Psychoanalytic diagnosis is less precise, and so psychoanalysts would call many patients borderline who would come under one of the other DSM-III diagnoses. In part this is so because psychoanalytic diagnoses often go beyond the descriptive features of syndromes, and may include assumptions about the nature of the pathology that are based upon developmental ideas and theories, and sometimes upon theories about the specific qualities of ego functioning in the different categories of emotional illness.

Freud himself never used the term *borderline* in his published work. He retained the view that there were two distinct categories of mental illness, neuroses and psychoses. He based his distinction chiefly on the preservation or failure of these patients' relationship to reality. In the early part of his career, he also postulated that psychotic patients suffer from a more severe variety of repression than do neurotics, in that they withdraw emotional cathexis from aspects of reality. He thought that this produces some of the symptoms of schizophrenia such as apathy and withdrawal, and that other symptoms such as hallucinations and delusions result from faulty efforts to make up for this problem. Freud always assumed that constitutional factors play a major role in determining who would develop one sort of illness and who another, but he also believed that the different forms of illness are probably based upon disturbances that appear at different stages of development. In his theory, and in the thinking of most psychoanalytically oriented psychiatrists and psychologists today, more severe forms of mental illness are the result of difficulties in the very earliest stages of development, while less severe problems result from developmental difficulties that occur later in childhood. As I will describe later in this chapter, there are those of us today, a small minority to be sure, who question the validity of this fundamental assumption about developmental level and the causes of adult onset of psychotic and neurotic syndromes. At this point, I will continue to follow the historical consequences of Freud's approach.

In his thinking, important pathogenic impacts on psychic development result in what he called fixation points at whatever stage of life either these psychological traumas, or other difficulties of a biological nature occur. Subsequent appearances of pathology are set off by biological and/or psychological stresses in later life; these produce syndromes whose form is in part determined by partial regressions of psychological functioning back to the levels that characterized the stages at which fixations have taken place. The earlier in childhood the crucial fixations occur, the more severe the form of later illness will be. In this reasoning he followed the medical tradition of seeking specific etiological causes for each disease entity. The current importance of Freud's theories about psychosis are not at all dependent upon the validity of his specific ideas about the mechanisms of psychotic symptom formation. It is related to the persistence of his idea that gradations in the severity of mental illnesses can be understood on the basis of difficulties that originally take place during certain specific phases of development, and on the fixations and regressions that are associated with those phase specific difficulties, although theorists of today do not use the same conceptual language that Freud used to explain their versions of this fundamental idea.

Even in Freud's own subsequent work, absolute diagnostic distinctions that were based upon the theory of repression, and of the patient's relationship to reality, were gradually replaced by an increasing appreciation of the tremendous complexity of psychological life, and of the advantage, or perhaps I should say the necessity, to pay attention to the vast and variable range of the subtleties of the entire spectrum of ego functioning. For example, we now know that patients' relationship to reality cannot just simply be categorized as either normal or pathological. We see that this aspect of the way the ego functions is quite variable, rather than constant, in healthy as well as in sick people. A person can be more or less accurately in touch with reality in one area of life, but not in others, and this can change from one day to the next one, and sometimes even from one minute to another.

While some of Freud's contemporaries and immediate successors tried to follow his lead and chart a precise correlation between stages and even substages of infantile development and later disease entities, as time went on, clinical observations made such simple connections appear less persuasive. As long ago as the 1930s some analysts and descriptive psychiatrists were recognizing a category of disturbances that was much more severe than the usual neuroses and milder character problems that are dealt with in outpatient psychoanalyses and psychotherapies. Yet, these sicker patients did not seem to progress inevitably toward psychotic decompensation of a schizophrenic or affective variety, even though they might have certain features that resembled those more serious syndromes. The concept of a borderline category, that lies between the psychoses and the neuroses, came into use, although even today there are differences of opinion as to whether this designates a true diagnostic entity, or only a vague description of a class of intermediately severe disorders of many different kinds, having few or no features in common. Even psychoanalytic clinicians who think that there are basic similarities in the pathology of all borderline patients recognize that there are many different types of such patients, with important differences in their manifest symptom pictures, and that these differences require explanation.

In the early days of psychoanalysis, case reports from the literature show that some of the patients being treated by the first generation of psychoanalysts were clearly psychotic. There were then, and there still are, a few hospital centers that are interested in applying a psychoanalytic psychotherapeutic approach to treating even the most severely ill psychotic patients. In part this grew out of the discovery that if you pay careful attention to the communications of even quite psychotic individuals, you can learn to recognize and understand the meanings of some portion of the content of their speech and behavior, especially if you are familiar with the nature of the unconscious mind and the elements of psychic conflict. As I mentioned earlier, at first even Bleuler greeted the discoveries of Freud with enthusiasm, because of their power to explain what, up until that time, had been altogether mysterious features of the behavior of schizophrenic patients. There then arose a number of different theories about the causes of psychosis that hypothesized that severe psychological troubles in the very early period of infancy, perhaps without even any contribution at all from biological predispositions, are what lead to the development of psychoses and borderline conditions. Although the different schools of psychoanalysis that had by then come into being each had their own somewhat different theories about how that takes place, they all seem to have focused attention primarily on the effects of the early environment that was provided by the mother, or other caretaking persons, upon the development of the infant and small child's psychological capabilities and vulnerabilities.

In America, H. S. Sullivan, one of the pioneers of the interpersonal school of psychoanalytic psychiatry, based much of his work on the observation and treatment of psychotic patients. In Great Britain, and later in Europe and Latin America, the influence of Kleinian psychoanalysis, and afterward of the British school of object relations psychoanalysis led by D. Winnicott (1958), W. R. Fairbairn (1952), and W. Bion (1957), among others, also gave rise to theories and treatment approaches about psychotic and borderline patients. Among the mainstream of Freudian analysts, both in America and elsewhere, the further study of the psychology of the ego was advanced by the work of many individuals, including some who concentrated upon the development of more severe forms of pathology. Some notable names you will encounter in the literature that deals with these problems include Helene Deutsch (1965), Heinz Hartmann (1939), Edith Jacobson (1964), Phyllis Greenacre (1952), Robert Bak (1946), Harold Searles (1965), Margaret Mahler (Mahler et al., 1975), Arnold Modell (1976), Otto Kernberg (1975), and many others as well. In recent years, the school of self psychology, founded upon the work of Heinz Kohut, has called attention to other types of severe psychopathology, especially of narcissistic disorders, that some psychoanalysts attempt to treat. It is beyond the scope of this chapter to describe in detail all of these important contributions, and point out the differences among the various theories and approaches to treatment.

Some of these theorists, and other contemporary workers whom I have not named, attach much importance to the part played by genetic disposition and other biological forces in the production of severe psychopathology, while others seem to think it is not so important as the psychological environment. Many think both are influential, but probably in varying degrees which are extremely hard to specify. In any case, all these thinkers have more or less followed the assumption that in cases of severe mental illness, it is likely that very early in development, before the onset of the oedipal period, which usually begins sometime around the end of the child's third year of life, something has already gone wrong. They believe that elements of the psychic structure that are essential for the proper development of the fundamental capabilities that underlie the integration of perceptions, the modulation of affects, the assessment of reality, the control of impulses, and consequently the nature of relationships with others, and perhaps even the basic quality of thought processes, are damaged by something unfavorable in the child's caretaking environment. Some of these analysts speak of defects or deficits in the formation of psychic structure, others of pathological forms of early object relationships, while still others conceptualize the basic difficulty or difficulties in other terms. A very highly simplified and summarized version of these theories could be stated this way: Profound failures in development in the first few months of life will lead to the severe psychotic illnesses that appear in childhood. Problems occurring after the first few months, but still in the first year of life, will greatly handicap the ability to form stable differentiations between psychological representations of the self and of others, thus predisposing those individuals to develop some variety of schizophrenia. If the developmental disturbance happens a little later, from late in the first year of life through the second year of life, as the gradual differentiation of self and object images or representations is going on, several varieties of pathological outcome are possible: affective disorders of psychotic degree, or any one of a variety of borderline conditions, or severe disturbances of self-esteem regulation. If the major traumatic influences come into the picture only later in childhood, then neuroses and neurotic character disturbances of milder degree are the likely outcome. The majority of psychoanalysts would probably also suggest that affective psychoses reflect a traumatic origin at a slightly earlier stage of development than do the borderline conditions and the more severe types of character problems. Most treatment that is either called psychoanalytic, or is based upon psychoanalytic principles, will be based on some form of these fundamental assumptions.

At this point I will present some questions about the psychoanalytic ideas about sicker patients that I have just summarized. A few theorists, like Charles Brenner and Jacob Arlow, have long expressed doubts about the phase specificity of the origins of mental illness. Clinical studies of psychoanalytic data in which I participated some years ago raised other objections to these various theories of etiology and treatment (Abend, Porder, and Willick, 1983). Recent work by colleagues who also participated in those studies, notably Porder (1987, 1990) and Willick (1983, 1990, 1991), will also be used to present to you some other ways to look at psychoanalytic contributions to the treatment of sicker patients. What I am about to discuss is not the viewpoint of the majority of psychoanalysts in the world today, but that of only a very small minority. Since I belong to that small group, and I believe these questions to be important subjects for future study, I will describe them now.

First of all, every psychiatrist is familiar with the fact that we have always had diagnostic problems when considering severely ill patients. Bleuler's (1911) early text referred to the group of schizophrenias, and generations of descriptive psychiatrists since then have argued about the definition of subtypes of schizophrenic psychoses. The same is true of the range of disorders classified as psychotic affective disturbances. Once the proposition that there are also a large class of borderline disturbances distinct from the psychoses in some respects was added to the diagnostic field, the possibilities for confusion were increased even more. As I have described, psychoanalytic diagnostic considerations are even more complicated than psychiatric ones, since they often go beyond the descriptive features of the syndromes, and add some of the assumptions about underlying psychic structure and even etiology to the picture. This has some value as a way of trying to differentiate between several possible sources of certain descriptive features that might look alike on the surface, but it also adds another element of uncertainty, because it makes the problem of verification more difficult, if not altogether impossible. One important consequence of these circumstances is that scientists have great difficulty in being sure that comparable patient populations are being studied and described by workers who report their findings and theories in the literature.

When the group of psychoanalysts with whom I worked some years ago examined the psychoanalytic literature on borderline conditions, we had great trouble in selecting the clinical criteria we should use for deciding which cases to include in our own study. We finally made up a list of general descriptive features of the borderline patients that excluded all propositions that are not clinically observble. We were interested in studying those borderline patients who could be treated with some success by psychoanalysis. The psychoanalytic treatment situation produces a different kind of data about patients' mental functioning than any other treatment situation can do, in that it is far more detailed and comprehensive in respect to observations of some aspects of how the mind works, especially in regard to the effects of the unconscious layers of the mind on thought and behavior. However, it is only suitable to apply psychoanalytic treatment to a small percentage of the sicker patients, and only a small number of patients can be studied because of how much time is required to treat each case with that method. When we published our findings, many psychoanalysts argued that we had worked with a patient sample that came only from the extremely healthy end of the borderline spectrum, while some psychoanalysts use diagnostic criteria that would not even include our patients among the borderline group at all (Abend, Porder, and Willick, 1983). When you think that nonpsychoanalytic psychiatrists may use still different criteria, and collect altogether different data, and that psychoanalysts of different theoretical beliefs all collect and interpret their data somewhat differently, it is not at all surprising that so much confusion still exists in our efforts to understand and evaluate sicker patients.

I will concentrate on some other problems in deciding about the validity of the various psychoanalytic theories about the sicker patient populations we study. There are many reasons to question the concept that specific developmental phases can be identified as crucial to the subsequent development of the different psychotic and borderline syndromes. For one thing, are we justified in accepting as reliable the assumption that the regressive symptoms and behaviors that are seen in adult psychotics and borderlines show us exactly how the mind of the child was working at the times of developmental disturbance and fixation? Today it seems more likely that at least some manifestations of the psychoses do not actually have a counterpart in normal early development. Studies of the withdrawal and deterioration evident in severe forms of schizophrenia, including childhood psychoses, cannot be regarded as providing precise reproductions of the mental states of infants in the first few months of life. Other manifestations of what are called regressive states may be the product of a primary biological disturbance instead. Furthermore, few psychiatrists or psychoanalysts have given sufficient weight to the possibility that some of the symptoms displayed by very sick patients could be psychological reactions to their awareness that they may be suffering from organic deficiencies. Both regressive aspects of mental functioning and psychological reactions to physical trauma are commonly found in patients with a variety of organic brain dysfunctions, including head injury, stroke, drug toxicity, and Alzheimer's disease. In fact, some primitive modes of thinking, and some pathological manifestations of childhood conflicts, will be activated by any form of physical illness, acute or chronic, especially if the brain itself is affected. If childhood psychological trauma and fixation plays an etiological role in such cases, it is more likely to contribute to forming the specific contents of each individual patient's mental preoccupations, than it is to produce the more general characteristics of the regressed mental state. Willick and others believe that in the past analysts may have been too ready to attribute psychotic patients' loss of distinction between their self images and their images of the outside world and other people to an underlying failure to develop this fundamental ability properly in early infancy. Neither current infant observation studies, nor reconstructions derived from life histories, or those based on analytic data gathered from the treatment of sick adults, provide enough evidence to confirm the theory of early life developmental failures as primary etiologic agents in psychosis. The same caution should be applied to the theories about what causes the borderline syndromes, even though the evidence in support of the importance of possible constitutional and biological factors in those diagnostic categories is not so clear and convincing as it is in the case of the major psychoses.

Deciding the question of what causes the pathology is not a simple matter, either in the case of the psychoses, or of the borderline conditions. It has been argued that hereditary and other biological factors, even if proven to be present, may not be sufficient to explain the latter appearance of these emotional illnesses. Perhaps, at least in some cases, these merely constitute predispositions that act to produce the critical vulnerability only when combined with some of the psychological factors attributed to deficiencies in the environment provided by the mother early in the child's life. It is even possible that the biological factors, if they are involved, serve to interfere with early psychic development only if they are present at certain critical stages. We do not know the answers to these important and difficult questions at the present stage of psychological and physiological knowledge. It is hard to imagine that if such severe early developmental disturbances are present, they would not manifest themselves in some ways, even during childhood and early adolescence, in those patients whose severe illnesses seem to begin only later on in life. However, we are learning that some hereditary and acquired illnesses can require many years before their effects are visible as manifest symptoms, so perhaps that could also be true of these severe emotional illnesses. At this point, we simply do not have definitive answers.

What I have presented is not intended to discount the idea that seriously disadvantageous emotional environments have harmful effects on the development of children, and that they contribute to the onset of the severe, as well as the milder, forms of psychological illness later in life. In fact, it seems entirely logical that the more deficient the environment, and the earlier in the child's development these deficiencies occur, the more profound their effects will be. Whatever damage may be done to the infant's capacities, or to those of the very young child, will certainly have effects on the way these individuals experience and cope with the inner conflicts and external challenges of later childhood and adult life. In psychoanalytic terms, the way each child meets the problems of its oedipal stage of life will be influenced by what took place earlier in its life, and by whatever damage, physical and/or purely psychological in nature, has already taken place. It is also true that events of a traumatic nature which happen later in childhood, or during adolescence or adult life, can also have serious consequences.

The viewpoint we believe in is that some of the patients in what psychoanalysts generally classify as the borderline group, especially some of those who show the milder degrees of borderline disturbance, can be treated successfully with the psychoanalytic method, or with modifications of it. Other, perhaps slightly more difficult patients can be treated with forms of psychotherapy that are derived from psychoanalysis, based on the psychoanalytic perspective on psychological development, and on the effects of conflict. Many psychoanalysts think that special forms of psychotherapy are necessary to treat borderline and narcissistic conditions, and some forms of severe neurosis or neurotic character pathology. Their theories of treatment are at least to some extent based upon their etiological theories, especially if they think that early stage specific damage has produced the particular defects or deficiencies in psychological organization they believe are at the root of the pathology. Our doubts about the validity of these theories about the causes of these conditions lead us to take a more cautious position. We think that severely damaged individuals, apart from whatever biological influences there may be, have probably suffered more severe environmental trauma all through their development, and that this psychological damage has more than simply certain stage specific effects. We doubt that their emotional problems can be understood and treated without also looking carefully into the consequences of infantile sexual and aggressive conflict, just as we study the effects of those problems in the psychoanalytic treatments of the less sick, neurotic individuals. In other words, in our way of thinking about the symptoms and treatment of borderline patients, we use the same basic organizing principles of compromise formation that we have been telling you about in previous lectures. We also realize that these sicker individuals have to be treated with a lot of patience and tact, if psychoanalysis or psychoanalytic therapy is applied. They are more sensitive than the usual patient in many ways, and have more difficulty in cooperating consistently in psychoanalytic forms of therapy. They cannot or will not talk as freely, they tend to demand more reactions and responses from their therapists, they are more fragile and labile in response to stresses in their lives, and in response to the stressful things that come up in their treatments. Their thinking may become more irrational, and their view of reality be distorted by defenses and by wishful thinking. They can be stubbornly blind to parts of themselves, and attribute to others, including the therapist, unacceptable or threatening aspects of their own minds. They can be very childish and inconsiderate, and even after making progress in treatment, they can quickly sink back again into illness. All this makes them very discouraging for even the most dedicated psychoanalyst or psychotherapist to treat.

Remembering and understanding the difficult experiences of childhood, and examining the ways in which these can be repeated in the analytic situation in relation to the analyst in the transference, are hard enough for the most stable, mildly neurotic individual to endure. It is all the more difficult for these sicker borderline patients to go through such treatments, and to gain strength from them. Progress in even the most favorable cases will be slow. Other, more difficult cases may not gain very much, even from extensive psychoanalytic treatments. Predictions for successful treatment are hard to make, and even experienced analysts are disappointed that some treatments they attempt do not turn out very well. On the other hand, we are also sometimes pleasantly surprised that patients who appear to be very disturbed emotionally can improve even more than we expect them to with the help of good psychoanalytic treatment. In some cases, what might appear to be only very slight improvements in psychological functioning that are brought about by careful psychoanalytic treatment can make a great difference to the patient's life.

I have not discussed the possibilities for better treatment of the sicker patient that combinations of psychoanalysis, or psychoanalytic psychotherapy, with various programs of psychotropic medication may offer. Psychoanalysts are not unaware of the potential for enhancing their treatment methods that new discoveries in the area of psychopharmacology are bringing to the world. We are just at the beginning of exploring these combined approaches. Even Freud guessed that the future might provide psychoanalysts with new forms of chemical treatment that could make patients who seem to be too sick for analysis to help become more accessible and responsive to psychoanalytic treatment. Many of us think that this part of his dream may also be about to be fulfilled. Still, there are and will be patients for whom psychoanalysis is not a good treatment, even with the concomitant use of medications. Other combined approaches may lie in the future, as will further advances in our understanding of the basic biology of all categories of mental illness. For the moment, I will leave the reader with the thought that psychoanalysis has contributed to our understanding of even the most serious forms of mental illness. It is best suited to exploring the psychological dimension, particularly that having to do with the effects of unconscious mental life. Psychoanalysts have little to say about the effects of biological factors,

and sad that he was not with her. This made some impression on her, but did not relieve the symptom. A few months later he also could see and explain that her feeling that he did not exist for her when they were separated was a form of expressing her anger. It was as if she were symbolically getting rid of him by getting him out of her mind and life, both because she was angry at him and also to protect herself from feeling how angry she was, or how lonely she felt. Gradually the symptom improved. Still later, when she had recovered more completely from these feelings and reactions, she could talk about them with greater freedom, and the therapist came to understand that the patient was also feeling very jealous when he was away from her because she knew that he must be with someone else, either another patient or his family. Finally she could understand and admit her childish wish that he would exist only for her, all day and every day, whether she was with him or not. These selfish wishes also made her feel very ashamed and guilty. Eventually she came to understand that the feeling that her therapist did not exist had been a way of saying to herself unconsciously that she wished he did not exist, or in other words that she was sorry she had ever allowed him to become important to her. Since she always knew that she could never really have him entirely for herself, she thought it was almost better not to care for him at all, so she would never have to feel so jealous, angry, sad, and lonely. I propose that this example demonstrates that although it may take a long time to uncover the hidden factors, it is possible in cases like this one to understand the childish, unconscious conflicted thoughts and feelings that produce such symptoms, even ones whose surface appearance may lead other therapists to conclude that they are evidence of some fundamental deficits in the psychic structure of the patient. The great advantage of working with the symptoms of sicker borderline patients as we have suggested is that the therapist is much more likely to look and listen for the underlying explanations of the symptoms than would be true if his theory leads him to assume that these symptoms are only manifestations of fundamental deficits in early development, instead of expressions of psychological conflicts.

References

Abend, S., Porder, M., & Willick, M. (1983), *Borderline Patients: Psychoanalytic Perspectives*. New York: International Universities Press.

Adler, G. (1985), *Borderline Psychopathology and Its Treatment*. New York: Jason Aronson.

Bak, R. (1946), Masochism in paranoia. *Psychoanal. Quart.*, 15:285–301.

Bettelheim, B. (1950), *Love Is Not Enough*. Glencoe: Free Press.

——— (1976), *The Uses of Enchantment: The Meaning and Importance of Fairy Tales*. New York: Knopf.

Bibring, E. (1954), Psychoanalysis and the dynamic psychotherapies. *J. Amer. Psychoanal. Assn.*, 3:745–770.

Bion, W. R. (1957), Differentiation of the psychotic from non-psychotic personalities. *Internat. J. Psycho-Anal.*, 38:266–275.

Bleuler, E. (1911), *Dementia Praecox or the Group of Schizophrenias*. New York: International Universities Press, 1950.

Bonaparte, M., Freud, A., and Kris, E. (1954), *The Origins of Psychoanalysis: Letters to Wilhelm Fliess, Drafts and Notes, 1887–1902 by Sigmund Freud*. London: Image Publishing Company, Ltd.

Bornstein, B. (1935), Phobia in a two-and-a-half year old child. *Psychoanal. Quart.*, 4:93–119.

Brenner, C. (1982), *The Mind in Conflict*. New York: International Universities Press.

Breuer, J., & Freud, S. (1893–1895), Studies on Hysteria. *Standard Edition*, 2:1–305. London: Hogarth Press, 1955.

Deutsch, H. (1965), *Neuroses and Character Types*. New York: International Universities Press.

Dostoyevsky, F. (1916), *Crime and Punishment*. New York: Macmillan.

Dowling, S. (1977), Seven infants with esophageal atresia: A developmental study. *The Psychoanalytic Study of the Child*, 32:215–256. New Haven, CT: Yale University Press.

——— (ed.) (1991), *Conflict and Compromise: Therapeutic Implications*. Madison, CT: International Universities Press.

Fairbairn, W. R. D. (1952), *Psychoanalytic Studies of the Personality*. London & Boston: Routledge & Kegan Paul.

Fraiberg, S. (1959), *The Magic Years*. New York: Charles Scribner's Sons.

——— (1977), *Insights from the Blind*. New York: Basic Books.

Freud, A. (1928), *Introduction to the Technique of Child Analysis*. New York & Washington, DC: Nervous & Mental Disease Publishing Company.

——— (1936), *The Ego and the Mechanisms of Defense*. New York: International Universities Press, 1966.

——— (1941), Infants without families. Reports of the Hampstead Nurseries, 1939–1945. In: *The Writings of Anna Freud*, Vol. 3. New York: International Universities Press, 1966.

——— (1963a), Assessment of childhood disturbances. *The Psychoanalytic Study of the Child*, 17:149–158. New York: International Universities Press.

——— (1963b), The concept of developmental lines. *The Psychoanalytic Study of the Child*, 18:245–265. New York: International Universities Press.

Freud, S. (1895), Project for a scientific psychology. In: *The Origins of Psycho-Analysis: Letters to Wilhelm Fliess, Drafts and Notes: 1887–1902*, ed. M. Bonaparte, A. Freud, & E. Kris. New York: Basic Books, 1954, pp. 355–445.

——— (1900), The Interpretation of Dreams. *Standard Edition*, 5. London: Hogarth Press, 1953.

——— (1905), Three essays on the theory of sexuality. *Standard Edition*, 7:135–245. London: Hogarth Press, 1953.

——— (1909), Analysis of a phobia in a five-year-old boy. *Standard Edition*, 10:155–318. London: Hogarth Press, 1955.

——— (1914), On narcissism: An introduction. *Standard Edition*, 14:69–102. London: Hogarth Press, 1957.

——— (1923), The ego and the id. *Standard Edition*, 19: 12–66. London: Hogarth Press, 1961.

——— (1924), The dissolution of the Oedipus complex. *Standard Edition*, 19:173–179. London: Hogarth Press, 1961.

——— (1925), An autobiographical study. *Standard Edition*, 22:7–74. London: Hogarth Press, 1959.

——— (1926), Inhibitions, symptoms and anxiety. *Standard Edition*, 20:87–156. London: Hogarth Press, 1964.

Furman, R., & Katan, A. (1969), *The Therapeutic Nursery School*. New York: International Universities Press.

Gay, P. (1988), *Freud: A Life for Our Time*. New York: W. W. Norton.

Goldstein, J., Freud, A., & Solnit, A. (1973), *Beyond the Best Interests of the Child*. New York: Free Press.

Greenacre, P. (1952), *Trauma, Growth, and Personality*. New York: International Universities Press.

Hartmann, H. (1939), *Ego Psychology and the Problem of Adaptation*. New York: International Universities Press.

Jacobson, E. (1964), *The Self and the Object World*. New York: International Universities Press.

Kempe, C. H., & Helfer, R. E. (1980), *The Battered Child*. Chicago: University of Chicago Press.

Kernberg, O. (1975), *Borderline Conditions and Pathologic Narcissism*. New York: Jason Aronson.

Klein, M. (1923), *The Psycho-Analysis of Children*. London: Hogarth Press.

——— (1975), *Envy and Gratitude and Other Works*. New York: Delacorte Press, 1975.

Kohut, H. (1977), *The Restoration of the Self*. New York: International Universities Press.

Kraepelin, E. (1913), *General Paresis*. New York: J. of Nervous & Mental Disease Publishing Co.

Lowenstein, R. M. (1957), A contribution to the psychoanalytic theory of masochism. *J. Amer. Psychoanal. Assn.*, 5:197–234.

Mahler, M., Pine, F., & Bergman, A. (1975), *The Psychological Birth of the Human Infant*. New York: Basic Books.

McDonald, M. (1970), *Not by the Color of Their Skin*. New York: International Universities Press.

Modell, A. (1976), 'The holding environment' and the therapeutic action of psychoanalysis. *J. Amer. Psychoanal. Assn.*, 24:285–307.

Money, J., & Ehrhardt, A. (1972), *Man and Woman, Boy and Girl: The Differentiation and Dimorphism of Gender Identity from Conception to Maturity*. Baltimore: Johns Hopkins University Press.

Piaget, J. (1951), *Play, Dreams, and Imitation in Childhood*. New York: W. W. Norton.

Plank, E. (1962), *Working with Children in Hospitals*. Cleveland: Western Reserve University Press.

Porder, M. S. (1987), Projective identification: An alternative hypothesis. *Psychoanal. Quart.*, 56:431–451.

——— (1990), On beginning with borderline patients. In: *On Beginning an Analysis*, ed. T. J. Jacobs & A. Rothstein. Madison, CT: International Universities Press, pp. 163–178.

Rado, S. (1933), Fear of castration in women. *Psychoanal. Quart.*, 2:425–475.

Robbins, M. (1983), Toward a new model of the mind for primitive personalities. *Internat. J. Psycho-Anal.*, 64: 457–473.

Robertson, J. (1952), *A Two-Year-Old Goes to Hospital* (Film: 16mm, b & w, Sound, 45 & 30 minute versions; English/French; Guide booklet). New York: New York University Film Library.

——— (1958), *Young Children in Hospitals*. New York: Basic Books.

——— (1968), *Jane, 17 Months: In Foster Care for 10 Days* (Film No. 2, 16mm, b & w, Sound, 37 minutes; Guide booklet). New York: New York University Film Library.

——— (1969), *John, 17 Months: For 9 Days in a Residential Nursery* (Film No. 3: 16mm, b & w, Sound, 45 minutes; Guide booklet). New York: New York University Film Library.

——— (1971), *Thomas, 2 Years 4 Months: In Foster Care for 10 Days* (Film No. 4: 16mm, b & w, Sound, 38 minutes; Guide booklet). New York: New York University Film Library.

——— Robertson, J. (1967), *Young Children in Brief Separation. Kate, 2 Years 5 Months: In Foster Care for 27 Days* (Film No. 1: 16mm, b & w, Sound, 33 minutes; Guide booklet). New York: New York University Film Library.

——— ——— (1971), Young children in brief separation: A fresh look. *The Psychoanalytic Study of the Child*, 26:264–315. New York: Quadrangle.

Rothstein, A. (1980), *The Narcissistic Pursuit of Perfection.* New York: International Universities Press.

——— (1984), The fear of humiliation. *J. Amer. Psychoanal. Assn.*, 32:99–116.

——— (1991a), Sadomasochism in the neuroses conceived of as a pathologic compromise formation. *J. Amer. Psychoanal. Assn.*, 39:2:363–375.

——— (1991b), On some relationships between fantasies of perfection and the calamities of childhood. *Internat. J. Psycho-Anal.*, 72:313–323.

Searles, H. F. (1965), *Collected Papers on Schizophrenia and Related Subjects.* New York: International Universities Press.

Seminov, P. V. (1986), *The Emotional Brain.* New York: Plenum Press.

Solnit, A. (1987), Book review of D. N. Stern: *The Interpersonal World of the Infant: A View from Psychoanalytic and Developmental Psychology. Amer. J. Psychiat.*, 144: 1508–1509.

Spitz, R. (1945), Hospitalism: An inquiry into the genesis of psychiatric conditions in early childhood. *The Psychoanalytic Study of the Child*, 1:53–74. New York: International Universities Press.

Steele, B. F. (1982), Effects of abuse and neglect on psychological development. In: *Frontiers of Infant Psychiatry*, ed. J. Call, E. Galensen, & C. R. Tyson. New York: Basic Books, pp. 235–244.

Stern, D. (1985), *The Interpersonal World of the Infant: A View from Psychoanalysis and Developmental Psychology.* New York: Basic Books.

Tyson, P. (1982), A developmental line of gender identity, gender role, and choice of love object. *J. Amer. Psychoanal. Assn.*, 30:61–86.

Willick, M. S. (1983), On the concept of primitive defenses. *J. Amer. Psychoanal. Assn.*, 31:175–200.

——— (1990), Psychoanalytic concepts of the etiology of severe mental illness. *J. Amer. Psychoanal. Assn.*, 38: 1049–1081.

——— (1991), Working with conflict and deficit in borderline and narcissistic patients. In: *Conflict and Compromise: Therapeutic Implications*. Madison, CT: International Universities Press, pp. 77–94.

Winnicott, D. W. (1958), *Through Pediatrics to Psychoanalysis*. New York: Basic Books.

Name Index

Subject Index

hereditary or acquired, on illness, and as yet little to say about how other approaches to treatment, as alternatives or as adjuncts to psychoanalysis, will affect the outlook for sicker patients. We are eager to learn more from our colleagues who study these dimensions of the problems we face together, and we think we have something of importance to contribute to their effort to advance the treatment of the mentally ill.

I will conclude this discussion of the psychoanalytic perspective on the treatment of sicker patients with a very short clinical illustration. I have taken it from a case reported by my colleague and co-worker, M. Willick (1990). I will describe one particular symptom that most psychoanalysts would agree is a typical borderline phenomenon. The patient, a thirty-year-old woman, began a psychoanalytic psychotherapy because of severe depression following her divorce. Although she quickly became quite dependent upon her therapist, she could hardly speak to him at all in her therapy sessions, and she did not improve, so after a time she decided to try with a new therapist who might understand her better. With the new therapist it was also very hard at first for her to speak to him about her thoughts and feelings. Again she immediately developed a very strong feeling of attachment to this new therapist, and she showed evidence of having very painful reactions to being separated from him on the days when no therapy sessions were scheduled. She told him that she was not even able to picture his face in her mind, or remember what he was like at those times. It was as if he no longer even existed for her. She sometimes would drive past his office as if to reassure herself that he had a real existence. Of course she always remembered exactly where his office was located, so this thought that he no longer existed for her must have stood for some complicated unconscious fantasies, thoughts, and feelings.

A number of analysts think that this type of development of a quick, intense attachment, and such unusual experiences as her report that she lost the memory of the therapist when separated from him, or her feeling that he no longer existed, are phenomena encountered specifically in borderline patients. Those analysts assume these to be consequences of an early deficit in the ability to sustain and integrate the emotional perceptions and memories of the self and others in a stable and reliable fashion. In other words, they think of this as a deficit in psychic structure. Analysts who follow that theory often adopt special measures in treatment, including permitting those patients to telephone them when they feel anxious, giving them a photograph of the analyst to help them reassure themselves, and giving those patients information about where the therapist may be found and contacted whenever he or she is away on vacation or at a scientific meeting. They think such steps are necessary to help these borderline patients make up for their structural deficiencies in emotional memory, and to help control the anxiety that results from this problem.

We think differently about such symptoms. We think that there are underlying unconscious psychodynamic reasons for these problems with memory and emotions. We would say that this problem is a severe impairment of the patient's mental functioning that is caused by the severity of the patient's conflicts, and not by some failures in the early mothering environment. Understanding the patient's conflicts can relieve this symptom, just as it can any other symptom. That is precisely what happened in the case I am telling you about. At first the therapist understood and explained to her that one reason she could not remember him was to protect herself, because if she remembered him clearly she would feel even more lonely